Throwaway Nun

Rosemary Scirocco-Corsale

With   Kathleen A. Barreca

Throwaway Nun   **Rosemary Scirocco-Corsale**
                      Kathleen A. Barreca

"Throwaway Nun" Copyright 2016 by Rosemary Scirocco-Corsale and Kathleen A. Barreca. All rights reserved. Printed in the United States of America; no part of this book may be used or reproduced in any manner whatsoever without written permission, except in the case of brief quotations embodied in critical articles and reviews. For information, address: kabarreca@gmail.com

The names, characters, places, and incidents in this book are the product of the author's imagination and are mostly used fictitiously. Any resemblance to actual persons, living or dead, businesses, events, or locales is entirely coincidental in the mind of the author... as is, whether it is fact or fiction.

First Printing 2016

Cover Design and Artwork by Mac McGovern
Copyright ©2016 Rosemary Scirocco-Corsale and Kathleen A. Barreca

ISBN-13:978-1530626632
ISBN-10:1530626633

Throwaway Nun

**Rosemary Scirocco-Corsale
Kathleen A. Barreca**

Dedication

To my parents, Joseph and Jennie Scirocco, and to my sister and brothers whose love and support smoothed my passage through a traumatic time.

In Memory of Scooter

I will never forget the day that she handed me this manuscript with a twinkle in her eye said you can read it now. I had known she was writing the book, but had no idea how close she was to finishing it. So on a cold, snowy Cleveland night I sat down and started to read my aunt's story of her convent life. Before I knew it, she was coming down the stairs laughing at me because I had never gone to bed; staying up and reading the whole book.

Years passed, still no book. Around 1978 she had a massive stroke that left her paralyzed on the right side; unable to speak, talk, or walk she entered rehab and like the fighter she had always been, she relearned everything she had lost. When my Uncle Joe crossed over she made the decision to move from North Royalton in Cleveland back to her hometown of Girard, Ohio where the story began.

Unfortunately her health began to deteriorate. She had gone from that scary lady all dressed in black, to a highly educated woman who spoke 13 languages and traveled extensively to a woman who had now made the decision to live the rest of her life in a nursing facility. As we cleaned out the house for the move she called me aside and handed me a large box. It was the book. On that day I made her a promise that after she had crossed I would do as she had asked and have the book published.

As I held her hand on that sad day in September of 2008, she winked at me and whispered, remember your promise. It was later that day she left us; all with our own memories of a very unique individual that I lovingly called Scooter.

It is now March of 2016; and with the help of a most kind hearted soul I am able to keep my promise. This is for you Scooter, your story; the story of "The Throwaway Nun"

I love you and miss you Scooter!

PROLOGUE

This is a true story. It is my story. No one could have possibly created the contents of these pages unless the incidents and occurrences were witnessed and lived. I did both. I lived eleven years of hell and the perpetrators have never admitted to a single fault. To have endured these personal horrors and escaped without apparent mental impairment may well be a miracle in itself. I am a much stronger person for having lived my teen and young adult years in this terrible place.

There is no intent to a base and degrade the Roman Catholic Church or the Vatican. They had no way of knowing what was happening. My story took place before Vatican II, before the medieval ways and methods of ruling religious were changed. The doors were opened after Vatican II and the abuses I sustained were no longer tolerated. The purpose of this book is not to discourage anyone from pursuing a calling to religious life, nor should any convent or monastery be judged by what happened during the time spent as a religious. The majority of current religious congregations would be shocked and appalled at what took place.

When I first tried to get the attention of the hierarchy of the Catholic Church in order to prevent others from being subjected to the horrors I lived with, I was called "stupid" because I did not leave of my own volition and it was said that I was a "disgruntled ex-nun." The early resistance and having the same humiliations heaped upon me played a large part in my choice to keep this story silent and never to pursue the matter; either legally or through the Church. I understood that it was a "no-win" situation.

Those with a background in psychology will be quick to analyze these pages and claim that writing about this phase of my life is "cathartic"; maybe so. To my colleagues and those who aspire I say: "Have fun with this book, nothing would please me more". The truth about my writing this book is not about "catharsis." It was started 30 years ago and I hesitated completing it because I never wanted the members of my family to know the details contained within these pages. I did not want anti-Catholic sentiment to be fanned and fueled. I have never sought sympathy or pity. I have not allowed myself time for either. However, in 1992, I was informed that the Daughters of St. Paul still think of Mother Pietra as a "saint," and following her funeral were collecting data to have her raised to the highest glory of the Catholic Church, canonization, I shudder at the thought. This book is a lasting record that in her lifetime she was an evil person, hiding her brutality behind the religious habit and surely brought her deeds with her to her judgment.

Those few who have heard part of my story always ask the same question: "Are you still a Catholic?" I am, but I did not practice my religion for 20 years! It was a long, long road to the internal resolution of my rage, the firming of my ego and self-worth, and learning the healthy parts of my anger and where to incorporate them. Transforming the self is not only a difficult task, but also a long one. Yes, I am a Catholic. Not only am I a Catholic, but I am a born-again, charismatic, practicing Christian-Catholic! It took years to know the spiritual truth for me. And I am happy! I am at peace inside, outside, and with the world. I have truly been blessed, and I am grateful.

As a Christian, the most difficult process in my conversion was forgiving those who had stripped me of my calling, caused me untold pain, and crushed the child inside. I continue to have to forgive every day. There are days in which I seem more forgiving than others. I determined long ago that I would never let anger rule my life or allow rage to run the motor of my accomplishments.

INTRODUCTION

In the center of the entrance corridor of the convent rested a huge pendulum clock which chimed the hours with a clear, heavenly bell. It was one of my many chores to tend to the clock, dust and polish the massive woodwork which encased it, then wind it with a large key reminiscent of those used in centuries past. With the glass-enclosed showcase of crucifixes, statues, books, and other religious items, it stood an impressive ten feet high. Across the top in ornate gold letters was inscribed, "Religious live the lives of angels." Perhaps the statement is true; however, my religious life was not like the angels. It was more like hell.

The bell had sounded at the end of the day and it was bedtime. Figures of women all dressed in black, exhausted after a hard day's work, floated slowly up the stairs; their veils weaving gently to and fro by their ascending motion. This night I was almost the last person to ascend the stairs to my room. My steps were slower than theirs and my exhaustion greater. I was ill. The sound of a rather subdued voice echoed with obvious tired effort the nightly prayer, "Virgin Mary, Mother of Jesus" repeated fifty times. And there was the response, "Make us saints," given in unison, also repeated fifty times. The scene was the nightly ritual and this litany was seldom said with much religious fervor, the responses were just as monotone and mechanical as a wind-up doll. But this night, June 21, 1958 was one which will remain etched in my memory for as long as I shall live!

I entered my room on the third floor as usual while responding to the litany in a low tone. I knew that these nightly rituals would soon end for me and my heart was heavy with anxiety and fear. I began to undress in the manner that nuns disrobe. Each part of the habit or religious garb carefully removed, kissed reverently, and placed on hangers ready to don the next day. As I turned to approach my bed, Sister Marietta grabbed my right hand. It was an unexpected action. I was startled at first, but did not pull away. She was crying and began kissing my hand. Her hot tears trailed between my fingers. In between sobs she kept repeating, "I'm so sorry."

Throwaway Nun

Rosemary Scirocco-Corsale
Kathleen A. Barreca

My hand had become wet and warm, and I can still feel the same sensations just remembering this scene. I was overcome with this display and it seemed a long time before I placed my left hand on Sister Marietta's shoulder and said rather simply, "What's wrong, Sister?" She looked up at me, tears streaming down her face, the look of sorrow and distress etched deeply in her delicate, fair features. In a faltering voice she said, "I just found out, Sister Fausta let it slip out; you're leaving the convent. Oh, I'm so sorry. You kept it all to yourself and you never let anyone know. Nobody could have guessed." I assured her that everything was all right and that I appreciated her concern. She took her hand towel and wiped my hand, which was wet from her tears, then gently let go of her hold.

I turned the light off and we both climbed into our beds. This unexpected scene and my own surprise repeated itself in my mind along with other anguished thoughts. Evening prayers had long ended and there was a nightly silence and stillness common to that hour in the convent. Then the silence was broken and Sister Marietta sat up in bed to address me. "Sister, are you asleep?" "No, I'm not," I replied. "Oh dear, I didn't mean to upset you and I know that you have to get a lot of rest. Please go to sleep, please." She was rather distressed. "Yes, I will, I will," I said, "I'm very tired—good night, Sister." There was a small sigh of relief from her and then silence again. I did not go to sleep for a long while. When and where and how had this tragedy of my life begun?

ACKNOWLEDGMENTS

 My thanks to John Sisko who, many years ago, stuck a microphone and a tape recorder in front of me and said, "Talk." To Sandy Copich who labored through the typing of the manuscript more than once.

 Special acknowledgments to Theresa Gabrielle Walsh, my dear friend, who not only encouraged me to write this book, but who sat near me for months, giving me courage, wiping my tears away, and helping me put pieces of my heart back together again.

 Thank you all!

Throwaway Nun **Rosemary Scirocco-Corsale**
Kathleen A. Barreca

Throwaway Nun Rosemary Scirocco-Corsale
Kathleen A. Barreca

PART ONE

For as long as I can remember, I wanted to be a nun. When I was a preschooler, I still vividly recall having a somewhat prophetic dream, which fired my imagination and became the inspiration for my religious calling. I dreamed that I was in a garden filled with a variety of brilliant flowers. I was standing before St. Rose of Lima (*for whom I was named*) and St. Theresa, the Little Flower of Jesus. St. Rose was holding a bouquet of roses and the Little Flower was holding a large crucifix. I wasn't afraid. I was spellbound by the beauty of these saints whose life stories I had heard many times. It was St. Rose who spoke and held out her hand to me. "You will be a nun," she said. That was all, nothing more, the statement delivered very simply, without elaboration. Then both of the Saints smiled and disappeared. I woke up. I must have fallen back to sleep because I recall, even now, looking around the room; it was very dark but I wasn't afraid. I felt very secure and happy. In the morning, I told my mother about the dream. From that day forward, I began to tell everybody that I was going to become a nun.

My parents immigrated to the United States from Italy. My father and mother were very devout, practicing Catholics. They were simple, hardworking people who believed in family cohesion, charity towards others, and giving those in need a helping hand. I was the last of their eight children. By the time I was born they had already buried three of their progeny in infancy; my oldest sister, Carmel, would die suddenly long after I entered the convent. They had undergone and survived many tragedies in their lifetimes and their faith and prayers sustained them. Although they were not religious fanatics, they taught their children deep

Throwaway Nun

**Rosemary Scirocco-Corsale
Kathleen A. Barreca**

religious beliefs and faith by their daily example. My parents were much respected people in our small hometown of Girard, Ohio, where over one-half of the population were immigrants like themselves; first-generation Italian-Americans. Of their five remaining children, I was the only one who attended parochial school and sang in the school choir.

While in elementary school, I went home for lunch every day with rare exception. My mother did not work out of the home and she was always there to greet me. My older brothers and sisters remained in school and at work, as did my father. In March 1947, I came home as usual for lunch. To my surprise, my mother was serving lunch to two nuns in our dining room, which was reserved for formal or special occasions. They were canvassing our neighborhood to sell religious books. They had been encouraged by my mother to stay for lunch. I could tell that my mother was happy (*for Catholic people, it was and still is an honor to have nuns and priests visit their homes*), but she was especially happy because they spoke her native language. I was so excited that I don't recall eating lunch. My mother had already told them all I ever talked about was becoming a nun. They talked to me about my idea; something they called religious vocation. I was enthralled by what they said, but even more delighted to hear that they accepted young girls at the age of thirteen. My birthday was only two and one-half months away and I would then be old enough to enter their convent. Most orders of nuns I had heard about or knew were teachers or nurses, but I always knew I wanted to become a missionary. The idea of going to minister to the natives and the wretchedly poor of foreign lands had always been my burning desire. I would qualify to join this Order in just a few short months and I was very excited. After this initial visit the nuns came frequently and stayed for lunch. When I got home I would talk to them and they began to tell me about their Order. These first visiting nuns informed us that they were founded in Italy before World War I. Their mission throughout the world was to engage in the apostolate of the twentieth century; they spread the gospel and word of salvation via the modern means of the press, radio, and movies. They also printed their own books and wrote the scripts for their radio programs and movies. They were the Daughters of St. Paul.

As their visits increased so did the talk about the possibility of my entering the convent during the coming summer. I can recall my delight, and began to spend more time in church on my knees in prayer. I couldn't wait for summer to come; I definitely wanted to enter the convent. I began to tell my friends at school what I was planning, but they simply looked at me in disbelief. After all, I was known as a real tomboy, mischievous, always willing to get into fights, even with boys. I was always ready to play for long hours, instigating my friends to steal ice chips from the iceman and green apples from the trees in other people's backyards. I was definitely not considered goody-two-shoes, or the "type" to enter a convent. Some parents didn't want me to play with their children because they thought I was a bad influence. When I finally entered the convent that summer, the whole town was in a daze and the event was the subject of many klatches, mealtime and over the fence conversations. Furthermore, I was amongst the first to enter religious life from that small town.

The Motherhouse of the Daughters of St. Paul was located on Staten Island in New York, across the bay from Manhattan. I had never been out of the state of Ohio and the very idea of the trip to New York City, which I had seen so often in schoolbooks and newsreels at the movies fascinated me and filled my days with anticipation. School

Throwaway Nun

Rosemary Scirocco-Corsale
Kathleen A. Barreca

dragged on and it seemed that summer was making deliberate efforts to avoid arriving. There were serious discussions with my parents. My older brothers and sisters were very opposed to the idea, protesting that I was too young and that I should complete high school before thinking about entering the convent. My parents offered no objections and thwarted my siblings' efforts at trying to change my mind. If my parents had any reservations, they made no mention of these to me or to the rest of the family. Their approval of my intention made me very happy.

In early July 1947, as I entered the Motherhouse of the Daughters of St. Paul I was accompanied by Sister Clara, one of the first two nuns who visited our home that fateful day in March. The train trip from Ohio to New York City was without incident. It was the first time I had ever slept in a train berth, and the excitement and anticipation robbed me of sleep that night. I occupied the upper berth and was glad that I had no need to use the bathroom.

The Pennsylvania Station in New York City filled me with excitement and awe; it appeared cavernous to my inexperienced eye. There were masses of people moving rapidly in all directions. Billboards with diverse advertisements filled the inside walls. Above the granite steps in the main lobby was a picture by Kodak that seemed to be the size of a house and hung so high that I had to tilt my head back to see it. It was overwhelming for a young, protected, small-town girl from the Midwest where everyone seemed to walk a whole lot slower and live their lives with a lot less confusion and speed. Nonetheless, my awe was to increase several times when we stepped outside. It was my first exposure to any building more than 12 stories high.

Throwaway Nun

**Rosemary Scirocco-Corsale
Kathleen A. Barreca**

We descended the steps to the railroad tracks beneath the pavement. Sister Clara explained that this was the subway and the quickest means of transportation in the New York City area. When the train was in motion, it was impossible to speak because the noise was so loud. It seemed as though the train was going at breakneck speed and we could hear the screeching of brakes long before entering a stopping point. Within a few minutes Sister Clara motioned that we would exit the train at the next stop. I remember walking to the Staten Island ferryboat looking upward and taking in this massive concrete sight. Sister Clara was holding my hand. I'm sure that I would have recklessly stumbled into people if she had not done so.

The trip to Staten Island was delightful. I had never been on a boat before. This one was huge and there were cars and trucks below deck as well as people. I have never ceased to enjoy that ferryboat ride both while I was in the convent and later during several visits to Manhattan. I can recall passing the Statue of Liberty for the first time. My feelings were of reverence and amazement. My mind seemed to flash through the myriads of newsreels at the movies, pictures in magazines and newspapers, as well as schoolbooks. Here, at last, I was actually seeing this great monument, this symbol of America! I was so overcome with these emotions that I think I wanted to cry. I remember saying something about this landmark to Sister Clara. She sensed my awe. "It's quite a sight, isn't it," she said. "Yes," I seemed to whisper, "I think she is beautiful!" I know that I did not cry; though I had moist eyes. I was still trying to take in all the sights and sounds that were so foreign to me, so completely different from the rest of my life's experience in our small Ohio town. I remember how surprised I was to discover that the Statue of Liberty was green instead of white as I

Throwaway Nun
**Rosemary Scirocco-Corsale
Kathleen A. Barreca**

recalled from the newsreels and pictures. I didn't dare ask why. A few months later I was to learn some of the history of the great symbol of democracy and freedom in the world. I learned that the statue was a gift from the people of France to the people of the United States to mark the allegiance of both nations. The statue had been cast in bronze and the salt water of the Atlantic Ocean, blown upwards by the winds, effected the color change. After that first sighting and the subsequent array of emotions, I was never to pass by Lady Liberty again without a sense of reverence, gratitude, and emotion. Throughout my many years living in the convent, I was never to have the privilege of visiting the monument and touring the inside of this American landmark until long after I left the Order.

The Motherhouse for the Daughters of St. Paul was located on a small hill, overlooking the bay near the ferryboat docks. I recall that we walked from the docks to the convent and seeing the convent for the first time left an indelible impression on me, which I hold to this day. Some of it was reminiscent of what I remembered from just visual and emotional kinds of images that portrayed a "convent." A wall of wrought iron and stone surrounded the grounds. At the entrance of the driveway stood large, wrought iron gates that remained open and enhanced the entry to the estate. The convent itself looked foreboding. It was very old; a three-story Victorian mansion with a large porch extending all around the sides which faced the bay. There was a circular driveway and a small patch of lawn to the right and to the left. In fact, it looked somewhat dreary and really looked like a place of seclusion and solitude. Upon entering, it was dark, quiet, and smelled of church incense. I was taken to the chapel immediately. After that, I met a few of the nuns. I was introduced to the

Throwaway Nun

Rosemary Scirocco-Corsale
Kathleen A. Barreca

Superior, Mother Pietra, who was to have the greatest impact on my religious life and was the major cause of my anguish. She was not very tall, but her voice was deep, and she commanded an authority and respect, which the other nuns never failed to, show her. Sister Clara kissed her hand; Mother Pietra smiled at me. They spoke in Italian and there was not much I could understand. My parents had taught me an Italian dialect which did not sound like the grammatically correct Italian which the nuns spoke. Everything was strange, and now my impressions and feelings were too. At that time, I did not experience any fear. I was still very young, still immature, and still trying to assimilate the newness around me. I did, however, feel very strongly that this was a turning point in my life and that I was to behave in more pious ways. The idea that I was shutting out the world, my family, and all mundane things was beyond my grasp at that age. I remember that I really did not know what to do next after meeting Mother Pietra and the other nuns. They allowed me to go outside alone to explore the surroundings. During this walk I became fearful for a moment while I thought about my parents. "Do they know where I am?" The concern passed very quickly. What took its place was a feeling of homesickness; I missed my family very much. I had never been separated from them and I felt so far away. At the same time there was a sense of my not being alone and of anticipation.

After lunch, I was told to take a nap. I found this very amusing because I had never taken a nap at home; however, I did as I was told. I was shown to the bedroom used by all the girls aspiring to become nuns in this Order. There were two others, also from Ohio. They were twins. I knew their hometown which was not very far away from mine. I was left alone to nap, but I didn't. Instead, I observed what this bedroom was like.

Throwaway Nun

**Rosemary Scirocco-Corsale
Kathleen A. Barreca**

This large room was very bright and airy, and held four single beds. Each metal, twin-sized bed was covered with a white spread and made up to look identical. The beds were topped by a metal canopy frame upon which white sheet-like curtains were gathered to be drawn at night for privacy. I never knew that religious shared bedrooms. All of my information gathered from books, movies, and the stories of the Saints reported that nuns and priests had individual cells, or rooms. These private areas are called cloisters, and visitors, even relatives of nuns or priests are not permitted to see or visit these private areas. I thought maybe that was only for aspirants and postulants. However, I would learn quickly that all of the nuns in this Order shared bedrooms. As an aspirant or postulant, we were forbidden to enter or look into the sleeping area of the senior nuns. One of the beds in the middle of the room would be mine. Sister John Mary, Mistress of Postulants, occupied the bed closest to the windows. My first naptime was spent exploring the room and every bed because they had not yet instructed me on the rules and regulations governing the cloister of the nuns compared to that of the aspirants and postulants. I noted the crucifix and two holy pictures on the walls. One was of the Virgin Mary and the other was of Jesus, the Divine Master. After this initial exploration of the bedroom, I looked outside the window which faced the bay. I could see the Manhattan skyline, the ferryboats, the tugboats, and a large freighter coming into port. If I close my eyes right now, I can still see that panorama; still feel my sense of awe and homesickness. I cried myself to sleep on the settee in front of that window. Sister Clara awakened me and I was taken to the Chapel to pray again.

It was in the early evening that I met the twins and the other nuns. They were arriving at the convent in pairs. They had been out all day selling books, something they called "propaganda." It was at this time that I discovered that the twins were only one and one-half years older than I was, and we got along very well. They had been in the convent for about one year before I arrived. I remember that they would giggle when I did something which was not cfe rigeur. I had a lot to learn.

It was at suppertime that I noticed a clear order of seniority. The refectory, or dining room, held two long tables parallel to each other. The nuns sat at one table with Mother Pietra at the head. The other nuns sat on either side in the order of their years of religious service. If there were any visiting superiors, they would sit nearest to Mother Pietra. Other visiting nuns sat in the order of seniority as the ones who remained at the Motherhouse. Since Staten Island was so centrally located and near the main ports-of-call for ships and the international airports, there were many visitors, nuns on their way to missions in South America, the Orient, and the South Pacific. Within the first year, I would come to understand that the Daughters of St. Paul on their way to these missions would be deliberately be routed through the United States so that the "Americans" would provide them with the necessities for opening convents in these distant lands. After World War II, the General Motherhouse in Rome was no longer able to provide either the means or support necessary in the opening of new missions. However, through the generosity of benefactors and the astute maneuverings of Mother Pietra, supplies for these missions were provided. Needless to say, this calculated generosity ingratiated Mother Pietra to Rome and made her indispensable. The aspirants and postulants sat at the other table with Mistress of Postulants occupying the seat at the head of the table. I was to learn that I was an "aspirant," that is a young girl aspiring to become a Daughter of St. Paul. Postulants were the

Throwaway Nun

Rosemary Scirocco-Corsale
Kathleen A. Barreca

young ladies who were of age to receive the habit, the distinctive garb of the Order. However, we were all referred to as postulants, and when we wrote home to our families, we used the word "postulant" before our first names. I was struck by how much older Sister John Mary, our Mistress of Postulants looked because she was so gaunt and thin. The twins and I teased her into telling us that she was 27 years old. (Nuns don't tell anyone their ages) And so, I became "Postulant Rosemary". I was? A few months into my thirteenth year, I had just completed the seventh grade of parochial school that June. This had been a long, unusual day for me; it marked the beginning of a long and unusual life!

There are many rules and regulations governing religious life and I knew none of them. Every day was a new learning experience. Every day one of the other nuns would tell me that this or that was not done in the convent, that I should not say something, should use better grammar, better words, and speak softer. Most of all they told me I talked too much and that I needed to learn to remain silent and use as few words as possible. I came from a very demonstrative, affectionate Italian family where everybody talked at the same time and said anything and everything they wanted. Neither my parents nor my teachers had ever told me that I talked too much, so this came as a surprise and left me with hurt feelings. I was too young to understand the "spirit" of silence in religious life. I was embarking on a life of personal and emotional rigor; a life which demands the most astute domination over one's every word and deed. But my spirit was still free in those first days. I was still innocent and unsophisticated. I wanted to learn with all my heart because I wanted to become a nun with all my soul.

Throwaway Nun

Rosemary Scirocco-Corsale
Kathleen A. Barreca

When I left for the convent my parents had given me a few items such as fruit, candy, and other sweets. I had been told to place these in the large, stainless steel refrigerator in the kitchen. The next day I went to the kitchen where Sister Sara was preparing the evening meal. I wanted a piece of candy so I opened the door of the refrigerator where I had seen Sister Clara place my goodies. As soon as I opened the door, Sister Sara stopped me saying that I was not permitted to go into the refrigerator without permission and was unable to have a piece of my candy. She seemed surprised that I would do so with that degree of freedom. I remember offering a weak protest informing her that I was not stealing anything, but just getting what was mine and that my parents had given these things to me. She patiently explained that nuns do not do anything without first asking permission to do so. I learned that I could not get a drink of water, use the restroom, take a bath, leave a room, or even go to the chapel to pray without first asking permission of another nun. From that day forward, I never went to the refrigerator again nor did I ever do anything without asking permission. However, if the Mistress of Postulants was present, she would grant the permission sought. The same order of seniority which I observed in the refectory was also observed in all other facets of religious life. I learned that I had to ask permission from a superior first, should she be in the room; next was the oldest of the nuns if Sister John Mary was not in the area, and so on. It was such an ingrained pattern for the other nuns that almost always permission was asked aloud and automatically the nun in the proper order of seniority would answer. Since every single action required permission, I was often stopped from doing something during those first days until I got it right. Permission was required even when I needed to throw away a piece of scrap paper or a

Throwaway Nun

Rosemary Scirocco-Corsale
Kathleen A. Barreca

tiny piece of sewing thread which could not be used. It was explained that securing permission for all things was an act of humility and submission. It showed obedience and a subjugation of one's own will. I could no longer think or act on my own; I was no longer my own person! Most of our talking began with "May I" and ended with "Thank you".

But the excitement and the whirl of new learning experiences were to come to a quick close. About two weeks after I had arrived in Staten Island, my parents called Mother Pietra insisting that I be sent back home. My mother had second thoughts about letting me go so young, and she insisted that I return home and consider waiting until I finished grammar school, at least, before returning to the convent. It was not until I arrived back home that I was informed that my oldest brother Tony had been prepared to come to New York to fetch me if I was not permitted to return. I was very disappointed in this turn of events; my parents knew that I always wanted to become a nun. They had no objections a few weeks ago and I could not understand why this was happening. I was sent back to Ohio by train accompanied by one of the nuns. We arrived first at the convent in Youngstown before going to my parents' home. They lived just minutes away. Once back home with my parents, I cried almost continuously because I wanted to return to the convent. I was unhappy with having to wait another year. I went to Mass daily, prayed on my knees often during the day the way I had been taught in the convent, and even spoke more piously than I had ever done before. I refused to go outdoors to play with friends. I refused to leave the house except to attend Mass. My brothers and sisters were very happy about my being back home. The situation vacillated like this for about three weeks, and then I got stubborn (*which was my old self*) and I told my mother that if they did not allow me to return to the convent, I would run away from home and they would not see me for a year! I think my mother believed me. She got frightened because she knew that I would probably do just that. The next thing I can recall is that my mother had prepared a big dinner and Sister Clara was present. My oldest sister hugged me and cried again, asking me to reconsider. I said goodbye to my family for a second time and I returned to Staten Island and to the Motherhouse. My religious life had begun in earnest and there would be no interruptions from this point onward. There was no turning back. My dream of becoming a missionary was to become a reality. I was happy!

My life as a postulant picked up exactly where it left off before returning to Ohio for those few weeks. In addition to learning things each day, there were religious practices which were part and parcel of the daily routine in the convent. As I had suspected, the world of nuns and monks in monasteries are governed by silence all the time except for periods of rest and recreation during which time we could speak. There was a period of "grand silence" from the time one finished night prayers until breakfast time the next morning. If anyone "broke" grand silence by saying even the smallest word in a whisper, the infraction required that the offender "consign" themselves to the Mother Superior as soon as possible. There are some religious orders and congregations which require that the nun or monk prostrate at the feet of their respective superior for a confession of faults. This was not the rule with the Daughters of St. Paul. At all other times, when permission was granted to break silence the tone was very hushed and words were few. The nuns were apprised of the beginning and ending of silences by the ringing of a bell. We were called to Chapel and to meals by the same bell. These were all easy to learn. Silence was not

Throwaway Nun
Rosemary Scirocco-Corsale
Kathleen A. Barreca

difficult to observe. There was a simple hand language that was employed to communicate. Everyone not talking meant there was no reason for me to talk. During our silences, one of the nuns would say an ejaculation; a very short prayer with an equally short response.

Within the first few days I was assigned a "number" which was to be sewn on the proper spot of every clothing item, including handkerchiefs. I was given "Number 2" and either the number alone or "N2" was sewn on to indicate that I was in the New York convent. It was followed by a small cross, the meaning of which was never explained, nor told to me when I finally asked. I was told that that was how it was done in Italy so that was how it was done in America. Sister Domenic, the nun who was assigned to that task, did all of the laundry. She was one of the sweetest nuns I have ever met in all of my life. After the laundry was done, everyone would help hang it out on the lines which were strung over the small plot of grass just outside of the back door. During the daytime, the laundry would be collected in bushels and placed in the refectory. After supper, everyone would help to fold the clothes, each item with the number showing. Then, stacks would be made and each person would collect their numbered stack on their way to retiring after nightly prayers. Nothing was ever ironed except handkerchiefs and the white, starched collars and head borders for the nuns. Postulants never ironed. We were not permitted to touch items of the habit relegated for use by the nuns only! We were permitted, however, to help hang undergarments on the line and to fold them when dry. It was not an unpleasant task. The laundry was hung out in the winter as well! Through the snow and sleet the lines were full; however, Mother Nature made no difference in her assault on people or clothing. When the laundry was retrieved, it was frozen and

Throwaway Nun

Rosemary Scirocco-Corsale
Kathleen A. Barreca

stiff! It was taken from the lines very gingerly and placed in the refectory on chairs and tables to defrost; it was done in Italy that way and the custom must continue!

Articles of clothing for both postulants and nuns were very different from those used by women (*even in other convents*). It was not until after Vatican II in the late 1960's when most nuns changed their looks and their habits and donned regular street clothes. That made it very difficult to differentiate many of them from those who were not nuns. Some altered their habits and shortened their veils or headwear. Gone, now, are the days of the heavily starched, white Wimples, the tight wrap-around head and neck pieces, and the voluminous skirts. But in 1947, nuns still looked like the now old-fashioned pictures. The style of undergarments of the Daughters of St. Paul came straight out of WWI Northern Italy. First I wore a long, over-sized, white undershirt which came to below my knees. The sleeves were about three-quarter length. Next, I donned a pair of bloomers which were loose fitting. The shirt hung out of the bottom of the bloomers at the knees. The bloomers had apron-like ties sewn on either end of the waistband, which were crossed in back and brought to the front and tied. The back "flap" resembled a pair of old-fashioned "long johns." They had a button on each side at the waist, and remained buttoned until I had to use the restroom. All I had to do was unbutton the back flap and drop the "trap door." Because they were hidden, the fabric used to make these undergarments were scraps of textiles of many colors and patterns. Often, several pieces of remnants were used for one garment! That's how it was in Italy! Over this combination came a dark brown full slip which was snapped down the front to the waist. The postulant's dress was worn over top of all this. It

Throwaway Nun

**Rosemary Scirocco-Corsale
Kathleen A. Barreca**

was a simple, black dress with two pleats on either side of the middle and had a hidden pocket on each side. The sleeves were long and had a cuff. The dress snapped in front from the collar to just below the waist. There was a fabric belt that fit loosely around the waist with one snap. A small, white "Peter Pan" collar was then placed around the neck and closed with a single button in front. Black stockings were worn by postulants and nuns alike, as well as black oxford shoes.

The first day I arrived, Sr. John Mary instructed me in the manner in which I was to disrobe at night. I was to reverently remove my dress, place it neatly on a hanger, and hang it in the closet. Next, I was to remove my shoes and place them beside my bed. I was, then, to get in bed, being sure to cover myself up to my chin, and remove my slip which was to be hung over the bed railing at the head of the bed. I was to proceed to take off my stockings and place them near my shoes without getting out of bed. Both the bloomers and the shirt remained; the other postulants, nuns, nor I had pajamas or nightshirts. The only other item of clothing worn by the nuns was a nightcap, which was white and tied under the chin. In the eventuality that I needed to use the restroom during the night, I was told to sit up in bed, don my stockings and slip, place my towel, which hung on the rail at the bottom of the bed, over my shoulders, and proceed to the bathroom. Upon my returning to bed, I was to remove the stockings and slip in the manner in which I had been instructed. We had no slippers, so I would have to wear my shoes, tiptoeing all the way not to make noise. Everyone else did the same thing, including the nuns. This is how it was done in Italy. In this old Victorian Motherhouse, there was only one bathroom on the second and third floors, and this was used by both postulants and nuns. Rarely, fortunately, did I ever have to arise in the middle of the night. However, if on any of those few occasions I would come across a nun also going to the restroom, I was to turn my back out of respect for her, since she was not fully dressed, and wait my turn. Much later, I learned that there was another bathroom attached to the master bedroom in the old house which was reserved for Mother Pietra and one other senior nun. No one else was to use that bathroom. I wore the same postulant's dress every day. I was given a "Sunday" dress which, as the name implies, was worn only on Sundays and holidays. My dress was never placed in the laundry to be washed. Instead, I was taught how to clean the soiled spots by using water, soap, and my towel. Stubborn spots were removed with cigarette lighter fluid and a rag used just for that purpose.

Although I wore my underclothing day and night, I was told that these were changed only once a week after my bath. I could ask permission to rinse out my stockings every night because these, too, were changed weekly. I tried that once and abandoned the idea when I donned wet stockings the next morning. The stockings were made of heavy cotton and did not dry overnight. Each postulant and nun was allotted one towel and one washcloth, which were hung neatly on the rail of the bed. These, too, were changed weekly. On Sunday night, the clean towels and washcloths were placed on the table outside the Chapel and everyone would take theirs to bed after night prayers. The bed sheets were also changed weekly. Only the bottom sheet and the pillowcase were to be placed in the dirty laundry. The top sheet was then placed on the bottom, and the clean sheet on the top. A clean pillowcase was given every week; and the process would cycle in the same way every week. Laundry was

Throwaway Nun

**Rosemary Scirocco-Corsale
Kathleen A. Barreca**

always done on Monday. Each Monday night, everyone's recreation was spent folding the clothes and stacking them as described earlier.

All of this I learned within those first few weeks. As I look back, I realize that there was much protocol and many practices to learn so quickly. I felt, from the beginning, that my life in the convent was supposed to be one of obedience and sacrifice. Not only was I going to become a nun and missionary, but I learned that I was also supposed to become a saint! In order to become a nun and a missionary, I was to observe all the protocols, religious practices, and rules and regulations. In order to become a saint, I was to suffer greatly. This was still beyond my scope of understanding. I knew that my saintly idols, St. Rose and the Little Flower, suffered very much.

They were persecuted and misunderstood by many around them in their daily lives and had sustained great physical suffering in silence. They had visions of our Lord and the Virgin Mary. They performed miracles, not only after their deaths, but while still living. They were not of this earth, I thought so often. I am of this earth and becoming a saint in their fashion was a thing of awe and of impossibility; I could only try my best.

Soon after my arrival, I was taken into the cellar of the convent. I was unprepared for what I saw! There were several different rooms off the small corridor at the bottom of the steps. In the corridor there was a commercial scale, a large freezer, and a small bathroom with just a commode. In the space under the stairs, there were rows of numbered hooks where both postulants and nuns placed their working aprons and half-sleeves, which we slipped over the long sleeves of our dresses and habits when doing even a small task. *(When doing very dirty work like scrubbing floors, shoveling snow, packaging boxes in the large garage,*

Throwaway Nun   **Rosemary Scirocco-Corsale**
                                                                                                           Kathleen A. Barreca

the nuns would hoist the sides of their habits and tuck them into their cinctures, or belts, from which also hung a long pair of rosary beads. The postulants' dresses were mid-calf and did not need to be hoisted.) In a large room to the left of the corridor was a storage room with piles and piles of various books almost as high as the ceiling. Off this room was a cold room for wine and food storage. The nuns made their own table wines each year. To the one side was the "steam room." The furnace had a small conveyor connected to it which brought the small coals into the center of the furnace, in turn, heating the water which traveled to the old-fashioned radiators throughout the old mansion. Old rusty buckets were used to put the ashes at the roadside for collection by the garbage men each week. To the right of the corridor were two large rooms. The farthest room had obviously been added to the mansion long after it was built because of the newer walls and the smoother cement floor. The first room held a machine which I was to learn was a book trimmer. The right side of the room was fitted with shelves to the ceiling. There were neat piles of books on all the shelves, and represented all the books produced and printed by the Order. These were in English, Italian, Spanish, and a few other languages like French and Portuguese. These books in foreign languages came from the convents of the Daughters in those countries where that language was spoken. There were work tables in the middle of the room where much packaging of mail orders and special requests were done. In the second large room there were other machines. There was an automatic stapler for small books, a "sewing" machine which stitched the backs of the book pages, and a large folding machine near the only window. The folding machine was huge and loud, and automatically folded large sheets of printed material which would then be sewn together

Throwaway Nun

**Rosemary Scirocco-Corsale
Kathleen A. Barreca**

to become the sequential, chronological pages of a book. There was no printing machine at this time. When I was shown about the workshop, known as the apostolate, Sr. Nazareth was operating the folding machine. A shipment of large, printed sheets had just arrived from the printing company. When each sheet had been folded by the machine, it represented 16 pages of a new book. Therefore, each set of pages were done all at once and then stacked and numbered. When all the pages had been properly folded, they would be assembled around a large table in the middle of the room and collated by hand. The large sheets were fed into the machine by fanning a small stack of the sheets and spreading them a bit by using an ivory bone the size and shape of a six-inch ruler with rounded ends. Powder was sprinkled on the sheets of paper to prevent sticking to each other, therefore wasting pages. At the other end of the machine these folded pages would accumulate until removed. This was the first job and task assigned to me in the apostolate: I was to collect the pages, make little stacks about four to five inches high, and wrap each little pile with a strip of scrap paper to which I had applied a dab of glue with a thick brush. These little stacks would then be piled high around the various rooms until all the pages were ready for collating. At first, Sr. Nazareth let the machine run at a slow speed so that I might learn the technique and rhythm of handling this job efficiently. I was a fast learner. The next day, I went to work again. This time she was able to operate the machine at full speed; I was fast at accumulating the pages and making the little stacks. In the meantime, I was observing what she was doing. I watched diligently as she turned the machine on and off, increased the output, and fanned the sheets into the feeder. I saw how she stopped the machine when there were doubles coming through and whenever there was a snag causing the sheets

Throwaway Nun

to get caught into the folding sections. I saw how she removed them; separating which could be salvaged and which would have to be thrown away. Very little was wasted. I became so proficient within a few days that Sr. Nazareth was often able to turn the machine on its fullest speed. I became very good at getting the little stacks to almost even inches high so that they could be stacked without too much difficulty. She taught me how to make the large piles, which I would do while waiting for the pages to accumulate. Actually, I was really running from one end of the room to the other. I was fully enjoying myself! I enjoyed doing this work and learning. I knew that this was what I would do for the rest of my religious life, and I wanted to learn it well. I had not yet, however, learned how to make this work "holy" by offering each page and each action performed for the salvation of souls, offering up each deed for the glory of God and Jesus, to withstand the long hours of standing and walking so that the Gospel, the Holy Word, would permeate the daily lives of souls all over the world. This I would learn, little by little, in the months and years to come. But at that time, those first few months of working with Sr. Nazareth at the folding machine were times of feeling good about doing a good job and showing those in authority that I truly wanted to dedicate my life to the Modern Apostolate. In fact, my ability and quick learning came to the attention of Mother Pietra. Once she came to the apostolate and watched for a short time. She was accompanied by a visiting nun and she commented on how well I was learning. That made me feel very good. I was, and still am, the type of individual who doubles their efforts when there is acknowledgment and positive feedback. My talent to be so proficient was rewarded by Mother Pietra telling me that I was to learn how to operate the stapling machine. After being told this, I was very

Throwaway Nun

Rosemary Scirocco-Corsale
Kathleen A. Barreca

pleased! I was happy that notice was taken of my honesty and effort, and that it was felt that I could contribute even more by learning to operate another machine. I was pleased at being offered the opportunity of taking on this "special" responsibility. I had yet to learn about humility and being low-keyed about such recognition. After one week had passed and no one had begun to teach me to operate the stapler, I began to ask and press for a specific time to do so. I came from a family where my parents never promised what they could not deliver and never said one thing while meaning the opposite. If my parents promised anything, I remember that they did not make us wait too long before making good on their promises. Then again, I am the youngest of their eight children, and there is no question that I often got the best my parents had to offer. There were so many older brothers and sisters to spoil me. At the same time this was happening in the apostolate, a group of young, American nuns had arrived from Rome where they had just completed their Novitiate, a year-long period of isolation, prayer, and study preparatory to taking the religious vows of chastity, poverty, and obedience. They also made the final act of discarding all worldly things by changing their own given Christian name. When a nun makes her profession of vows, she becomes the "Bride of Christ," in a spiritual sense. There was not, at that time, a Novitiate in the United States for the Daughters of St. Paul, and this was the first group to go to Rome for Profession after the Second World War. One of them, Sr. Anita, took over the operation of the folding machine. During non-silence times, I had told her about Mother Pietra telling me that I would be taught to operate the stapler and that I hoped this would happen soon. One day after lunch while the nuns and postulants took a short walk around the grounds and the porch, Sr. Anita turned to Mother Pietra and said, "What

Throwaway Nun

Rosemary Scirocco-Corsale
Kathleen A. Barreca

is wrong with this child? All she does is ask, when she is going to learn how to operate the stapler." She said this in Italian, and though all I knew at that time was how to speak in the Neapolitan dialect taught to me by my parents, I understood what she said. Mother Pietra then turned to me and said, "You will not learn to operate the stapler!" I was stupefied! I didn't understand what I had done wrong to merit this punishment. I could not understand why Sr. Anita would have reported my asking this in such a negative manner. Why was I being so severely humiliated? I remember my heart leaping up to my throat, my pulse quickening, and my face flushing. These were the same kinds of feelings I felt so many times during the seven years I attended St. Rose School in Girard. After only a few months in the first grade, we were told to bring a pair of our father's or older brother's old socks to class the next day. Upon entering the classroom, there was sawdust and chips of special wax on the floor. We donned the old socks over our shoes and were instructed how to slip and slide on the floor to polish the oak planks. During class, we rubbed our feet under our desks. At recess, we slid up and down the aisles and across the front and back of the classroom! A classmate took my hand and we went sailing up and down the aisle, unable to stop! We struck the pedestal upon which was a small statue of the Blessed Virgin Mary. It came crashing to the floor and disintegrated into hundreds of pieces before our very eyes! Both of us just stood there paralyzed with shock and fear. Sr. Virginia, an Ursuline nun, scolded me, placed all the blame on me, and told me that I would have to bring $5 to her to replace the statue. I was horrified! My heart was beating right in my little throat, my pulse quickened until I was sick to my stomach, and I felt my face flush. I couldn't understand why I was the only one being blamed for the misdeed.

Throwaway Nun

Rosemary Scirocco-Corsale
Kathleen A. Barreca

I thought my parents would surely give me a beating. But, I confessed my crime to my parents telling them exactly what had happened. They did not punish me, but gave me the $5 which I delivered to Sr. Virginia's hands the next day. The incident must have set a pattern for me at St. Rose School. There were other incidents for which I would be blamed unjustly throughout the seven grades I attended there. In the fourth grade, the class was having a special "May Day" in honor of Our Lady, and the students were to bring candles to hold during a little procession in the classroom before the crowning of the statue of the Blessed Mother with a small band of fresh flowers. I brought two candles to school. One of the other girls did not have a candle, so I gave her my extra one. Once we had lit them and started to line up for the procession, she turned to me and whispered that the candle was shaking because it was broken in the middle. We exchanged candles at the very moment Sr. Dorothy turned her head to hear me say, "Here, take mine." I was scolded before the entire class and was made to sit silently at my desk for the duration of the ceremonies. The girl never came to my defense and Sr. Dorothy did not believe my explanation. During my last year at St. Rose School, we were practicing for the elaborate procession which would mark both the opening and closing of the annual Adoration of the Blessed Sacrament. All the girls in the seventh grade were in the choir and Sr. Marie, our teacher was the choir director. I sang soprano, and had a very good voice. However, for the procession, we were lined up in order of height with the shortest girl first and the tallest girl last. I was in the middle in front of my cousin, Delores, who was a smidgeon taller than I. On this particular afternoon, we had gotten in the wrong position for our dress rehearsal. I tapped her on the shoulder and whispered that we had to trade places. Sr. Marie had just walked up the

Throwaway Nun   Rosemary Scirocco-Corsale
                                    Kathleen A. Barreca

aisle and saw me with my head turned toward Delores. She called me out of the line and told me take off the satin cape, leave it on the seat of the last pew, and to go home. Furthermore, she stated that from that day forward I would not be a member of the choir; and, I never was. The following summer I would go into the convent and never sing again at St. Rose Church. Again, I experienced the same rush of feelings. No one came forward to explain the truth about the incident. The nuns really ruled with fear. The other classmates surely felt that if they came to my defense, they would be ejected from the choir, as well. Months later, I was asked to join the choir for the celebration of the new pastor's thirty-third birthday. It seemed that J was the only one who could hit the high "C" note in the special song. I refused, telling Sr. Marie that if I could not sing for God, then I would not sign for the pastor. She looked stunned, but never said a word. So here I was a postulant in the convent and starting a new life! Weren't these nuns different? Weren't they supposed to be living the lives of angels, and all becoming saints? It was grade school all over again. I was being punished unjustly all over again. My heart was breaking, and I remember not saying a word. I was gripped with a feeling of heaviness, of gloom. I was too young and immature to read the "signals" then. I should have spoken up and defended myself. It was an omen of things to come.

Summer had ended and preparations were being made for the academic year. The twins and I were the only ones attending high school classes that year. Although our school work and grades were sanctioned by Cabrini Academy in Fort Washington, New York, we never attended classes in that private, all-girls school. Instead, all classes were taught at the Motherhouse by Sr. John Mary and Sr. Nazareth. Sr. Renata would teach the Italian language, which was more compulsory than all the other subjects. She also taught Latin, which was essential since all Roman Catholic Liturgy was in Latin, the language of the "church" throughout the world. We attended classes and study periods all day, with a break for lunch. During the entire three years I spent attending high school classes, I was the only student in my grade. The twins were one grade ahead of me. The only classes we had together were religion, history of the Catholic Church, and other similar religious instructions. I was privately tutored all through high school. Since there were no classrooms at the Motherhouse at that time, classes and instructions were held in the postulants' bedrooms, the infirmary, and the special room where the nuns counted the money collected daily from their propaganda. Postulants were never permitted to be in the vicinity while money was being counted. It was during the preparations for the academic year that I was informed that I would start the ninth grade. I had just completed the seventh grade at St. Rose School and had been promoted to grade eight when I entered the convent. So, I would be skipping the eighth grade altogether. I was somewhat apprehensive because I was never good in math and knew that I needed the materials taught in the eighth grade in order to be able to understand and complete the algebra courses required in New York State. I was assured that I would get the extra help. I was good in spelling, history, geography, art and civics. I was not apprehensive about skipping the last year of elementary school in these subjects. And so it came to pass that in September, 1947, I started the ninth grade of high school. I never graduated from elementary school.

It was not long into the academic year that I began to have problems. It is now so long ago that I cannot recall the precise reasons for my being hauled into the office of Mother Pietra on a regular basis. My

Throwaway Nun
Rosemary Scirocco-Corsale
Kathleen A. Barreca

closest recollection is that I got off the subject in the one-to-one classes, didn't learn the academics as quickly as they thought I should, and didn't complete all the homework given. Another reason was that the completed themes and written assignments did not please the tutor. Only Sr. Nazareth, who taught algebra, history, and science, ordered me to Mother Pietra's office. She would stand outside the office door and listen to every word. In the office I had to stand directly front and center of Mother Pietra's desk. She would begin verbally chastising me, but not so much for my non-feasance or malfeasance of school work. She degraded my personality, calling me disobedient, lacking in humility, and not having the necessary spirit and soul to become a nun. Then, she would always use the singular "nerve spot" which would cause my soul to wretch. She would talk about my saintly and good-hearted parents and what a disgrace I was to them and to their good name. She threatened to either call them on the telephone to tell them how bad I was or to send me home to live the rest of my life being despised by my wonderful family and the community. My stomach would be raveled in knots; my face would flush as I did all I could to fight back the sobs and tears. In the beginning of these "sessions," I cried until my body shook so as not to have the sobs escape. My head was always held down. After a few more times, I simply held my head down and succeeded in holding back the tears and the shaking. During the first verbal tirade from her during which I did not cry, Mother Pietra seized the opportunity to further wrench my heart and soul, to instill even more fear and fright. She told me that I was not crying because I was not paying any attention to what she was telling me, and that I lacked even a small semblance of humility. According to her, my not crying was showing my defiance to holy obedience, to the spirit of

Throwaway Nun

**Rosemary Scirocco-Corsale
Kathleen A. Barreca**

humility, and self-abnegation. When I had cried, she accused me of being proud and disobedient, of being non-attentive to her words. I was confused. It seemed that whatever I did would not be the correct action. I could do nothing right. At no time did she ever ask me for some response, nor did she ever take into account my feelings or what my thoughts were. I had been in the convent less than three months when these "sessions" began. This was the beginning of many such humiliations done both in private and in public before all the other nuns and postulants. It was the beginning of hell!

Before I went into the convent, I had been a very spirited young girl who did above average in school, had a great sense of curiosity about life and everything in general. I had more than a little talent in art, music and singing, and was a hard worker. I always felt sorry for the "underdog" and had many fights with schoolmates on that account. In that same vein, I often went to ask the question, "Why," if I didn't understand something. Neither my parents nor my parochial school teachers had ever considered this an act of disobedience. My parents and teachers knew that if I got praise for something done, I would double my efforts and try to do much more in order to please. I like being happy and making other people happy. My parents were very charitable and generous people, and I liked to follow their example of helping others in need. That doesn't mean that I was an angel sprouting wings. I could be stubborn, difficult, and act very spoiled. I disobeyed my parents and, in retrospect, realize that I was not an easy child to rear. My older brothers and sisters had been far more compliant than I with their wishes and were less prone to barrages of questioning when something didn't suit their fancies. My endless energy, being in constant motion, and my enthusiasm for savoring everything in

Throwaway Nun

Rosemary Scirocco-Corsale
Kathleen A. Barreca

life gave both my parents and my older siblings' more than one headache. I was far more outspoken than most young children of that day. However, I also observed the goodness of my parents. Frequently, they initiated a clothing drive for a neighbor who suffered a catastrophe like a house fire or loss of a job. They often fed the homeless who came to the back door for food. They shared in the bounty of their victory gardens with those in need, both family, and friends. I almost always accompanied my mother when she went downtown Youngstown on Saturdays to shop for clothing and household items. I would often annoy her by pleading for money to give to each and every beggar along the streets. There were the blind, the amputees, and the bedraggled who offered a pencil or a small ruler in exchange for a donation. I never took their offerings. It was not until years later that these needy disappeared from the shopping areas of many towns. At that time, the welfare system as we know it today was yet to come. So while I was a "feisty" youngster, I had compassion for those less fortunate and those in need. I was sparked by going into the foreign mission field and doing even more to help "heathen souls and pagan babies." My childish mind and body were often stubborn and immature, but my heart and soul already belonged to Jesus.

It was this simple yet complex, active, immature youngster who entered the convent. My passing through convent doors did not alter my personality, nor did it make me mature beyond my years. I brought the totality of myself to religious life; that is, a totally committed, still immature, active 13 year old girl whose zest for learning and life did not cease. There was a sense of awe about religious life; a part of me that knew my parents were proud and happy about having one of their offspring dedicate their life to God and Church. There was a part of me

Throwaway Nun

Rosemary Scirocco-Corsale
Kathleen A. Barreca

would grow to be different as I studied, waited, and prayed to really become a religious nun, to become a Bride of Christ. But I was still at the beginning point when I was ordered before Mother Pietra for the "sessions." There is no doubt that she saw the zest, the enthusiasm, the willingness to learn, and the great desire to become a nun. She noticed the lack of sophistication, and the deep respect which I held for my parents and family. She saw the need to "kill" this free spirit, to subdue the curiosity and questioning into blind obedience, to squash my inquisitiveness by humiliation and mortification. She used threats about my family to squelch any objections I might have proffered. She used my immaturity and simplicity to instill fear. She used her position of superiority to demand blind obedience. Having learned to obey and never to question, she could then through the years systematically and thoroughly destroy my self-confidence, all vestige of self-worth, and any notion that I possessed any intelligence or talent. She could kill the spirit; she could try to kill the person. She had many helpers, and there was, for the next eleven years, no reprieve and little respite.

My life-long desire to become a nun was so strong that I never thought about requesting a leave to return home. I knew from the readings about the lives of the saints that one had to endure misunderstandings, physical, as well as mental pain to achieve sainthood. I knew that I was supposed to be obedient in all things so I never protested their treatment of me. I knew that I had to subdue my will, so I did not try to save myself from the humiliations and degrading. I knew that I had to work hard in all areas: school, the apostolate, and household chores; in order to cleanse my evil, bad soul, in order to be worthy to remain in the convent. In an early religious conference given by Mother Pietra, she had informed the postulants that if we ever decided to leave the convent, we would become Protestants, prostitutes, and would be damned to hell forever! I was very frightened because I wanted to become none of the above! It was easy for her to perforate my defenses and intimidate me. I was young, impressionable, and without having yet developed the sense of "total self" and "coping mechanisms." I was easy prey and an even easier "whipping post." There was never any thought that the nuns could be wrong, that their judgment might be prejudicial, or that they might act as mortal human beings. Having held nuns in awe all of my life, I continued to do so considering them holy women who were special in the sight of God and mankind. They were special because of their vows, the years they had dedicated their lives to the Lord, and the rejection of all mundane things. At that time, I thought they had the ability to read my mind and my heart, and that they were not evil nor had evil intentions. I felt they were above other humans, and their hearts were pure. It would take at least two and one-half years before I became fully aware of the "humanness" of religious; like me, they had faults, made mistakes, were unkind, and suffered from the "human condition." Since they were missionaries and talked about humane attitudes toward those not Catholic; the heathens and pagans alike, I never dreamed that they would not practice the tenets of the Gospels, in the spirit of piety and of saintliness. Their haloes were very tarnished, but it would take me years to discover the hypocrisy.

Hence, it was from the beginning of my postulancy that Mother Pietra and the senior nuns began to consider me semplice, an Italian word meaning simple or like someone from the backwoods! I would not verbally retaliate in any situation where I was being raked over the coals. The nuns also began to think I had no feelings, no heart, and no reasoning

Throwaway Nun

Rosemary Scirocco-Corsale
Kathleen A. Barreca

power. I was ripe to be molded and formed the way they felt best without thought to the inside person still with growing pains. I tried to be obedient, I tried hard to be mature, and I tried even harder to practice all the advice given me. I wanted Mother Pietra to find me worthy of my religious vocation.

I remember one particular occasion when I was brought before Mother Pietra for one of our "sessions." That day, she was especially brutal with her words and threats. Sr. Nazareth remained, as usual, in the corridor outside the office. When I exited to return to class, there stood Sr. Nazareth—almost in my path. We looked at each other squarely in the eyes. I saw a strange look on her face which I will never forget. Not a word was spoken. I thought I saw a glimmer of compassion. For the remainder of my convent years, Sr. Nazareth was one of the handful of nuns who never caused me grief! It was more a question of having all the senior nuns get into the act of raking me over the coals for what they considered any small issue, any human error, and anything they thought I could endure. The other teachers in school also took to handing down more advice and corrections about my composure, habits, and the do's and don'ts, than about my attending an academic class. The senior nuns, who were not my teachers, found no difficulty in daily corrections and advices. And so each day passed, one following the other, none being different than the day before.

It was during the first three months that I was allowed to accompany a senior nun into the community to sell books. It was a Saturday and there was no school. Sr. Renata, my Italian language teacher, was the senior nun. We went into a residential district in the Borough of Bronx. We visited families living in the tenements along the street. There

Throwaway Nun

**Rosemary Scirocco-Corsale
Kathleen A. Barreca**

were no elevators, and we climbed to each floor knocking on each door. Most were not at home. When we reached the top floor, we would descend. Going down was much easier than going up! Stopping on each floor was like a rest. Each nun carried a large, black satchel in which books, leaflets, and pamphlets had been placed the previous evening. Sr. Renata had a large bag and I had a smaller one which held fewer books. It would not be until later than I, too, would carry a large satchel. When selling books in tenements and single-family homes, it was customary to ask a "good family" if we could stop and eat our lunches in their homes or apartments. By "good family," the nuns meant very warm, receptive people, always Catholic. Usually only one or two people were at home at the lunch hour. It was a plus if the family was from Italy or they were of Italian descent. Without exception, the family felt very honored to host the nuns, often offering to prepare lunch rather than eating the lunch that was prepared at the convent. On the first floor of one tenement building, Sr. Renata found a lady who was home alone and was very warm. She was so pleased to have us in her home. She offered us something to drink and Sr. Renata, accepting for both us, agreed on hot tea. In my parents' home, tea was something taken or given to my siblings or me when we were ill with the flu, bad head colds, or just feeling seasonal "blahs." It was served with honey and a shot of whiskey. Drinking hot or even iced tea was a new experience for me, but I obeyed without objection. However, in an effort to be helpful and pleasing to the "good sisters," she added sugar and cream. My lack of tact and grace reared its ugly head and I mentioned that I had never drunk tea with cream in it before. The lady was quick to want to replace the tea with sugar only, but I held on to the cup and saucer protesting that it was fine. The more the lady insisted that it would be no

Throwaway Nun   Rosemary Scirocco-Corsale
                                                                            Kathleen A. Barreca

problem to make another cup, the more I insisted that the one she had already prepared was good enough. Finally, the lady relented and Sr. Renata's face flushed beet red. However, I can still remember the taste of the tea and my mild surprise that it was so good. On most occasions, to this date, I take hot tea with cream. It all started in that first-floor tenement. What I never got used to was the sight of unwelcomed visitors and inhabitants of many New York City tenements. Sr. Renata and I were seated at the small kitchen table, which was placed against the wall. We sat opposite each other eating our lunch and drinking our tea. In the midst of the meal, a cockroach gingerly wound its way up the wall. It decided to change course from its route and began coming toward me. Seeing the bug didn't frighten me, but I did not want the cockroach to fall on me or my food. I moved my chair away from the wall. At that precise moment, the kindly lady turned toward us and saw the intruder. She was immediately embarrassed and became apologetic. Sr. Renata made light of the matter, but her face was flushed. With lunch over, we both thanked the lady for her hospitality and left to visit other tenements to sell our religious books. When we came out of the building, Sr. Renata reproached me about my behavior and told me how nasty I was. She said I should have remained still. I could remember asking, "What if it had fallen on me?" She replied, "You let it fall on you and don't do a thing!" Mother Pietra heard the report from Sr. Renata, who told of the incidents blow by blow. It would be many months before I was allowed to accompany a senior nun again into the community.

    Weekdays were occupied with attending classes. The sessions had stopped, and it seemed I got along much better in school. I found that algebra was very difficult for me, but other subjects were easier. I had

Throwaway Nun

Rosemary Scirocco-Corsale
Kathleen A. Barreca

learned to speak fluent Neapolitan dialect from my parents; now I was learning "Classic Italian," the grammatically correct language. My letters written to my parents in Italian were improving and my parents were pleased. During the fall months of 1947, letters were laced with phonically written words in dialect amongst those I learned in class each day. By the end of the first year, I was able to read, write, and speak Italian with a modicum of facility. I understood most everything except for those words not indigenous to our everyday conversations. As postulants, we wrote home to our parents and families once a week. The letter-writing was done in the classroom on Sunday evenings. Only one letter was permitted each week. Permission had to be granted to write more often; I know that very few ever did. When the weekly letters were written and placed in addressed envelopes, they were given to the Mistress of Postulants. Every letter was censored and if the Mistress or Mother Pietra did not like the contents, even one line, the letter was given back to the writer with instructions to rewrite it. Censorship of both Incoming and outgoing mail was in effect throughout my convent years. If we were to receive any money in our letters, the amount would be written on the outside of the envelope. Whenever packages were received from home, either the Mistress or Mother Pietra was present when it was opened. No one ever got to keep whatever the family or relatives would send. On one occasion, I received a package containing a bed quilt and two down pillows. I never saw them after the package was opened. It was not until years later that I learned that they had been placed on Mother Pietra's bed! I was permitted to keep the black shoes, boots, and gloves sent to me. Throughout my eleven years in the convent, my parents bought me every pair of shoes I wore except for a pair of Italian shoes which were too small. This was not

Throwaway Nun

true of the other nuns, postulants, and aspirants. The convent supplied them with their footwear.

Mother Pietra was the ultimate authority in all matters. She not only reigned supreme, but she relished her power. From the very first weeks in the convent, I was told that every Daughters of St. Paul in the United States owed much gratitude to her because of the many sacrifices she had made to establish the Order in America. Respect for her was almost a revering of her, and Mother Pietra never hesitated to flex her muscle to keep all the nuns allied and in fear of her. Everyone kissed her hand when greeting her, upon arrival from any of her trips, or, as I would learn, to secure a favorable position with her. So it was a normal course to have any of the senior nuns "reporting" or gossiping to her about each other or the postulants. To encourage this unchristian like behavior even more, she would pretend to seek their advice and/or opinion about matters relating to the convent or its operation. Mostly, they discuss what actions she might take toward those who were perceived as not fully agreeing with her. Even casual comments, not intended to be abrasive, were reported to her. Hence though Mother Pietra might be far away, she had developed a secure net of informers. No one wanted to displease her; no one wanted to be the object of her disfavor. On more than one occasion, she sent nuns back to Italy because they did not agree with her or because they would write to Rome about what they perceived as actions not in keeping with the original spirit of the Order. In the course of my 11 years, I would observe her sending many young girls back home.

One of Mother Pietra's favorite things to do was to make the sign of the cross on our foreheads and then "pretend" to make it stick with a small tap on the same spot with her fist. I saw other's actually grovel for

Throwaway Nun

Rosemary Scirocco-Corsale
Kathleen A. Barreca

this sign from her. Somehow, I never gained enough favor with her because whenever she came to plant the cross on my forehead I could barely feel her finger graze me. She was always sure never to tap me with her fist, but merely made it appear so to others. On almost every occasion, I would look her directly in the eyes; I can never recall her looking back at me. In fact, throughout my convent years, rarely did she ever confront my eyes. For many years, I thought these kinds of "avoidances" were because of my unworthiness and stupidity. In retrospect, I wonder if she, even in those early years, knew that I knew of these charades. Could she see, then, that I would gradually learn of all the hypocrisies?

Besides learning through school and through the various ways of correction and humiliation, there were more intense means of achieving what was said to be avenues of spiritual growth. Every month, there was a day-long retreat, usually on Sunday. During this retreat, it was customary to meet with the Mother Superior or Mistress for a conference lasting from 15 to 30 minutes. This was known as "passing." The first months were very instructive and educational. Soon, these passing's became ugly and downright cruel! I was denigrated, belittled, made fun of, and mentally tormented. On more than one occasion, especially when getting "passed" by Mother Pietra, she would get so loud that others could hear her. More than once, one or the other of my peers would privately comment on these events. They would ask me why I took this kind of treatment and why did I not stand up for myself; most never commented.

From the beginning of my religious life I was instructed to take notes on all retreat lectures and "passing's" regardless of who my superior was at the time. Those early notes are filled with prodding's and urgings to be "obedient" to all those in authority but especially to superiors. I not

Throwaway Nun

**Rosemary Scirocco-Corsale
Kathleen A. Barreca**

only took notes but I read and reread them often. It was no wonder, then, that I did not defend myself or seek to redeem my qualities; those in authority knew better than I did and I dared not contradict them.

I had already learned the hard lesson of crying; I had already learned the hard lesson of trying to reason. What was left for me was to remain silent. After all, I was being taught every day that suffering in silence, learning blind obedience, never questioning the authority of superiors (*their authority was directly from God the Almighty*), being humble enough to take criticism, never to say anything if anyone hurt us with words or actions, I was taught that these were virtues and the qualities inherent to good nuns! I was too immature and too innocent to realize then that these silences, never reacting negatively to the constant barrage of unjustified reprimands, the constant deprecation of my person, and allowing public humiliations were sending those in authority a loud and clear message: they could do with me what they wanted, say whatever they wished, and punish me with their mean words because I would never be contrary. I would take the punishment, and I learned how to cover up my feelings very well. My face would never tell tales. I was quickly learning to internalize these myriad negatives. These negatives would, in turn, fortify my ever growing lack of self-worth and dignity, and in turn I grew to actually believe that I was the worthless, most ungenerous, and most unworthy individual to ever have a vocation to religious life. I grew to expect the worst; it never failed me. It was only when I had made my vows that I learned that others would talk back, reply, refuse to accept corrections, and often, the directives given them by the superiors. For me, it was too late; the pattern was set, and I had no guidance out of the mire. As I look back, I often wonder how many times the superiors' verbal

Throwaway Nun

**Rosemary Scirocco-Corsale
Kathleen A. Barreca**

scathing followed on the heels of those who rebelled. I made for a wonderful whipping post and scapegoat.

Notwithstanding, I continued to keep cheery, to be spirited, and to be helpful to others. Rarely could I allow myself to show any moodiness or emotion. If ever I did, I seldom escaped the confrontation. Again, my immaturity showed its ugly head; this continuation of cheeriness and spiritedness was interpreted by the superiors as my inability to internalize anything they said and to practice their directives according to obedience. No one ever thought I might have feelings, I might have emotions, or I might be suffering inside. After all, I was only 14 years old. No one ever asked. Anything I ever had to say was dismissed as exaggeration, lacking truth, and had no merit. Less than one year after entering the convent, I began to be called a number of unkind, soul-crushing names. One of the favorites was mammalucca, meaning retarded one or nerd. I was often called stupid, forgetful, distracted, ridiculous, and not worth anyone's time. I was called one or more of these names almost daily by those who professed to be the "Brides of Jesus," HIMSELF! These names were used from 1948 until 1952, when I received the religious habit of the Order.

It was in 1948, one year after I had entered the convent, that an incident occurred that I recall as though it had happened just yesterday. I already mentioned that I was very fond of my family and that I wanted them to be very proud of me. Hence, they were never told of the type of treatment I was receiving in the convent. Since our mail was censored, there was never the opportunity to tell them. They had no way to know my degree of suffering. Nonetheless, soon after the start of the school year in September, 1948, I was ordered by Mother Pietra to write a letter to my parents and tell them just what it was that I did that I was so bad as to have

Throwaway Nun

Rosemary Scirocco-Corsale
Kathleen A. Barreca

to write home about it. It would seem that if I were so unruly, they would promptly send me home and tell me and my parents that I did not have the stuff it takes to be a religious. That never happened, but write the letter I did. It was censored by Mother Pietra herself. Much to my chagrin my father wrote me back. The letter was written in Italian and I was made to read it while Mother Pietra watched. I wanted to cry, but I waited until I went to bed that night. The letter from my father read:

"Dear Rose:

I'm responding not to your letter because Angie has already written to you, but to one word which you said and that 'I am still a disobedient.' You know what disobedience is! Disobedience is rendering one's self similar to Satan. Satan embraces disobedience; he cultivates and nourishes it in order to make one a companion of eternal perdition. And you, under that holy roof, instead of making yourself closer to whom you have dedicated your life, you try to separate yourself from Him with disobedience. What do you think Mother Pietra thinks of us? And what does she think of you? What value is a vocation without obedience? What value is charity without obedience? What value do good deeds have without obedience? How would faith and the "armies of the Lord" be directed without obedience, which is the foundation? Jesus Christ died on the cross to obey His divine Father; and who are we but little worms? Which examples have Baby Jesus left us by subjecting Himself to two human beings of His own creation? What would you feel in your heart if Mother Pietra told you that you no longer could remain in the convent because you do not have a vocation? And if she were to say to you, 'Go home,' how painful for us! Please, I beg you for the sacred wounds of

Throwaway Nun

Rosemary Scirocco-Corsale
Kathleen A. Barreca

Jesus Christ throw yourself at the feet of Mother Pietra and ask her pardon for your acts of disobedience. Throw yourself at the feet of your confessor and tell him everything. Throw yourself at the feet of the good sisters and ask their forgiveness, because even they are your elders and you owe them obedience. Do penance and ask to be enlightened by the Divine Paraclete, so that you may persevere in your resolution to be worthy of the habit that you wear. For God's sake I ask you enter into yourself and know that Jesus Christ has picked those who must propagate the Holy Gospel, and you, who for divine grace have entered into that holy place where those with holy ideas convene, how dare you to stray from the right path! When your superiors speak, God speaks! We pray for you.

May this sweet reprimand be for you indication and courage for a new life. Your superiors have the right to be obeyed and respected. All of you work for one goal. Make me happy and promise me that from today onward, with the grace of God, you will be humble and obedient. Our only joy for us, and with it our thanks, is that God has not only selected you, but one from our family has departed and become a disciple to work in the vineyards of the Lord! I expect a letter from you in which you will say that you have repented and that you are obedient. This letter that I write to you is in secret and I will not make anyone of the rest of the family know because they know nothing of what I have written and of what you write to tell me; so please write a few lines in Italian. We are all well. Our greeting in Jesus Christ.

Your father,

J.S.

P.S. Please have Mother Pietra read this letter.

Throwaway Nun

Rosemary Scirocco-Corsale
Kathleen A. Barreca

To this day, I still do not know what terrible disobedient act I committed to be forced to cause my parents to worry and to cause them that kind of pain. My father never knew how mortified and humiliated I was made to feel. His letter only fueled the growing repertory of Mother Pietra and the other nuns too enmeshed in her ways to contradict her. This would be the first and only such letter I would be forced to write home. I would never be forced to cause my parents any worry again. In fact, neither my parents nor my siblings ever knew anything was amiss for me in the convent until after I returned home ten years later. Just reminiscing, just going back and pulling into my conscious memory what I put behind, what I buried for so many years is an extremely painful process.

You can imagine the kind of impact this made on me and my emotionality at receiving a letter like this from home. I knew that this would be cutting to my parents. They could not have had any idea that I had been coerced to write the letter in the first place. Nor, could they have had any idea of all the problems and duress that I had been experiencing. Many years later when I was to leave the convent, my father was to recognize all of those things and he would be extremely hurt. The pain came to him; not only that I had been submitted to all of this, but due to the fact that not by God, but by mere mortals I was being denied the perseverance in a religious vocation. He was to die very shortly after my leaving the convent without ever realizing some vindication for his daughter whom he felt needed and deserved it. His own feelings were made manifest not only to the family doctor, but to his parish. He had been encouraged by several persons to present the problem to Rome! However, his own plans had died with him and I never followed suit in presenting anything to Rome. I felt that this would be useless and that Rome would

Throwaway Nun

Rosemary Scirocco-Corsale
Kathleen A. Barreca

do nothing. They would not believe such a story. The attitudes and conduct of those who professed to be consecrated to Jesus, Himself, were so reprehensible, so incredible, that I doubted Rome would believe this story. I doubt if they would believe it now. This is not something that was created in my mind; I endured it! It happened! Other nuns witnessed this—it is truth! This is my story. While I appeared to be the main scapegoat, there were others who were victims as well. If anyone dared to disagree with her will and wishes, they would incur Mother Pietra's wrath. Over the years, I had occasion to witness her verbal lashings against some of the senior nuns. Several of them had their turn to go to Italy for family visits and refused to return to the United States! They could not sustain the oppressive tyranny of her rule. No one formally protested against the injustices, with the exception of one, my five co-novices left within four or five years of my departure. Everything that I endured there is part of me now. I certainly feel that I'm much more sensitive to other people's problems as a result of what I've gone through.

During the first two years of aspirancy, completing the academic work for one's high school diploma was to take precedence over all else during the weekdays. On the weekends, we were permitted to go out to sell books and other religious tracts with the senior nuns. Each evening, several nuns would gather in the kitchen after the evening meal's dishes were washed and put away to prepare the lunches for the nuns going out the next day. Each lunch packed had two sandwiches of meat, lunchmeat, or cheeses and one sandwich of jam, jelly, or peanut butter and banana. The bread, which was baked there, was cut in very thick slices. These unusually large lunches were accompanied by a fresh fruit. They were put into brown lunch bags and placed in the refrigerator. In the morning after

Throwaway Nun

Rosemary Scirocco-Corsale
Kathleen A. Barreca

breakfast, the large tray holding the lunches would be taken out and put on the table. Each nun would take a bag and place it in her black, cloth bag which lay atop the satchel of books. The rule was that if you brought any part of your lunch back to the convent in the evening, you had to finish it with your entire supper meal. One would think that everyone was very obese with all this eating, but very few nuns were overweight. When I entered the convent I had a weight problem, and these enormous portions only helped me put on more pounds. I was never scolded for leaving anything on my plate, and there were a few nuns who looked approvingly at any second helpings that I would request.

We never fasted in the convent. We were instructed quite early that the Daughters of St. Paul were missionaries and did manual work, and therefore, were dispensed from fasting with the exception of the Lenten Season; Fridays were strictly adhered to as meatless. I never learned how to fast, how to keep the oral sense in control, and that continues to remain a problem to this very day. There was never a dearth of food. There were three very hearty meals a day. Some nuns were assigned to do the cooking and to bake the bread. I was never assigned to the kitchen and never learned how to cook. However, I remember how good the food was and how plentiful. On Sunday, there was always some kind of pasta asciuta, which is macaroni or spaghetti with a meat sauce. There were never any meatballs. Then we had oven-baked chicken cooked in white wine. I really wished I had that recipe now; I can taste it still these many years later. Next, we ate potatoes or another vegetable. Everyone had to eat a minimum of two slices of bread per meal. Homemade wine was taken at lunch and at supper. One of the fathers of the nuns would come to Staten Island every year to make the wine. The barrels would be stored in a special, cold space in the cellar. It was good wine. This wine, however, was never used at the altar. The wines used during the liturgy were purchased and reserved strictly for use on the altar.

It would not be for several years before I learned that all the food eaten was never purchased; it was all donated from a variety of sources. For instance, there was a wholesale chicken market on Long Island. Once or twice a month, the nuns would go there and the wholesaler would stuff one, two or three live chickens in the black, cloth bag. These chickens were not marketable because they had broken legs or wings or some other defect. When the bag was filled, it was taken to the convent's station wagon which had two empty, wooden coops in the rear. The chickens were placed in the coops. Several trips were made from the market to the coops. When the coops were full and/or when all the wholesale merchants had been canvassed, the coops were taken to a poultry shop owned by some very generous man who would dress each of the chickens. The proprietor would then place them back in the coops wrapped in white paper. While the chickens were being dressed, the nuns would go elsewhere to sell books or visit other markets where foodstuffs were donated. There were wholesale vegetable markets, fish markets, docks, and large import companies which were regularly visited to receive donations. Generally, items donated were not sellable because the case of canned goods was damaged, or the large tins were without labels or crushed. Vegetables were also damaged. The nuns would gather in the kitchen to clean and glean these legumes whenever it was "market day." So, the menu was often predicated by what was donated. People were very generous and kind to the nuns. I am not sure that they knew they were collectively feeding an entire community, and then some. Occasionally,

Throwaway Nun　　　　　　　　Rosemary Scirocco-Corsale
                                       Kathleen A. Barreca

there would be an announcement made in the morning at breakfast that potatoes, cake mix, sweets, or fruit was needed. The nuns who left that morning to sell books would return in the evening with the requested items, often there were duplicates of the items requested, but none were ever wasted. If a fruit was rotted on one side, that would be cut out and the good part saved for fruit salad or baked fruit. It was the same with vegetables and meats. There was one occasion when this preserving and not wasting was taken to excess. I was told to bake a cake for Sunday dessert. The Mother Superior handed me a boxed cake mix and when I opened it, I saw worms and I brought the box to her to show her the problem. She took the box from me, strained the mix through a sieve, threw out the worms, and ordered me to proceed with baking the cake! There was a strange odor emanating from the oven while the cake baked and it did not rise. The strange odor was even stronger when it was cut and served. Everyone ate their piece silently, except for one nun who complained that it was inedible. Another time a large tray of ice cream bars, sandwiches, drumsticks, and Italian ices were brought from the freezer. Everyone was encouraged to "make a sacrifice" to the Lord and take more than one piece. The taste was very stale. Within hours one of the twins, myself, and one or two nuns got hives and were ordered to take a bath with Epsom salts. Nuns believe that this strict adherence to not wasting anything was dictated by their vow of poverty. However, I do not recall a repeat of such incidents after the ice cream party. These excesses, in the name of poverty, were not confined to food items. There were practices that were so outlandish that they often did not make any sense. We were allowed to wash our hair only once a month during the summertime. The postulants were given Okite, a granular laundry detergent, to use in place of shampoo. Carrying the vow of poverty to the extreme was also shown in the use of donated black shoe polish, which was dried out and crumbly from age. So that the chunks of polish would not mark the floor, we would polish our shoes on newspaper. Other donations of personal hygiene items that we had to use were dried out toothpaste and hard bars of soap with cracks in the edges. This soap was also used when Okite was not available for shampooing our hair. The Daughters of St. Paul are one of the few orders of nuns that do not cut their hair. Nuns braid their hair and wrap the braid in a bun at the nape of the neck. Postulants and aspirants braid their hair and wrap it around their heads from crown to nape. Hairpins keep the braids in place. It is difficult to justify the practice of not shampooing frequently when these women had long, braided hair. That is why there was much rejoicing when we were permitted to go swimming; our hair would be "washed" more often.

During the winter, no one was permitted to wash their hair because it was thought that wet hair would cause a cold. (*Such was the thinking in Italy.*) I am sure that there are those who suffered greatly from this strict, unhealthy practice. In fact, I remember one such instance during my novitiate, I shared a room with two co-novices. One morning, Sr. Maria took off her night cap in preparing for the donning of her cap and veil. I saw a layer of crust all over her head. Dandruff flakes clung to strands of her hair above this layer. To my knowledge, nothing was ever done about this condition and the shampooing practice continued long after I left the Order.

      Personal modesty was disregarded relative to the use of sanitary napkins. Squares of flannel or cotton cloth were issued to each of the nuns in lieu of sanitary napkins. These would be washed out by hand or left to soak in basins of cold water, which were placed under the bathtubs. Often, more than one person would have their soiled clothes soaking in the same basin at the same time. If a nun was going to be out for the day selling books, she would take several of these cloths with her. After changing, she would place the soiled cloths in a bag, which were to be washed upon her return to the convent. We were instructed that this unhealthy and unsanitary practice was necessary to save water. It is common knowledge and a fact of history that until the 20th century, women used diaper-like cloths during their menses.

However, the Daughters of St. Paul were founded just before World War I and while they continued to use cloths instead of sanitary napkins, this practice continued in the United States because that's how "it was done in Italy." In the 1970's, approximately twenty years after I had left the convent, I learned that the nuns were finally using sanitary napkins. The ex-nun who told me this reported that she asked Sr. Constance why this changed. She replied that the commercial napkins were more sanitary and more modest. Another example of unreasonable daily practices was the procedure for using the bathroom in the schoolhouse. The toilet was only to be flushed after all of the postulants waiting in line to use the facility were finished. It was flushed once in the morning and once at the end of school.

The habits and veils were never washed. Rather, stains would be removed with cigarette lighter fluid, and the habits would periodically be turned inside out and brushed. The cap worn under the veil was laundered once a month.

Upon awakening each morning at 5:30 A.M., everyone was given a half an hour to use the bathroom, brush their teeth, get dressed, and

Throwaway Nun

Rosemary Scirocco-Corsale
Kathleen A. Barreca

make their beds. At 6:00 A.M., a bell rang to call everyone to chapel for morning devotions. The water used each morning was cold. The convent had no mirrors for use. One towel and one washcloth were used for an entire week. After bathing they were hung each morning on the foot rail of our beds. Once a week, we were permitted to bathe in the bathtub. However, not more than two inches of tepid water was to be used. When the nuns menstruated, bathing in the tub was prohibited; in Italy, they said it would make one sick.

Every year, the Daughters of St. Paul would have a bazarre or a festival in late June. After the religious liturgies, the attendees would bring their own picnic baskets and dine on tables scattered throughout the convent grounds. For months prior to this festival, all recreation time allotted to the nuns and postulants was immersed in making up the small papers with "#10" into rolled scrolls. This was done with knitting needles and each scroll was secured with a grommet. On the porch which surrounded the convent there were wooden shelves, and in front of the shelves there were barriers which were draped so that no one could reach the shelves but the nuns working behind the barriers. All the "prizes" on the shelves were donated items from combs, rulers and such to large things like a toaster, frying pans, toys of every description, and myriads of kitchen, gardening, personal, and gift items. Each of these items had a "number" pinned or taped to it. The scrolls with #10 were not winning numbers. However, one could redeem ten of the #10 scrolls and get a comb, ruler, or other junk prize. Each scroll cost ten cents. There were always two nuns selling the scrolls which were kept in large glass jars with openings big enough to allow any individual to reach in and get his or her own number of scrolls. The most coveted of all the prizes were the

Throwaway Nun
Rosemary Scirocco-Corsale
Kathleen A. Barreca

beautiful baby dolls. There would be screams of delight when a person would win one of them. But what the public did not know was that the method of assigning the "big-prize" numbers was a very crafty one: only one handful of winning-number scrolls was placed in each large jar! Only one number for a doll was put into each jar. These numbers were controlled by Mother Pietra herself, and she would be the only one to put the winning numbers in the jars. When considering that the jars were the five-gallon size, one can immediately see that the unsuspecting attendants to these festivals were the objects of a ruse. It was very similar to the raffle which was held at the same time. The names would be drawn in front of all; however, if the winner were not present then those prizes would be given to one or the other of the benefactors with very clear agendas....either to get more money or donation of goods from one, or to bring back a donor who might have not been generous that year. So, it was all very calculating. These actions were justified as using every means to bring glory to the Lord! I thought this behavior very unusual that first year. I never questioned this rationale; I was learning to obey without question. These annual festivals were very profitable, even though I never learned how much money was made. Since nothing was purchased, all funds taken in were gross gains. I know that the total sum had to be in excess of $2,000 just based on the scrolls and raffle tickets sold. In the late 1940's, this was a great deal of money!

Shortly after this festival, the first one I ever attended since my arrival at the convent, I was ordered to go with Sr. Mary Basil to a foundations factory in New York City. It seems that during the festival someone had commented to some of the senior nuns that I looked very fat and pregnant. Therefore, the idea of a corset seemed appropriate. What I was given was a corset with iron stays and steel hook-and-eyes. There were long, thick laces that were tightened and then brought around to the front for tying. I wore this corset for the better part of one year. That same year, I was given a small vest-like garment to wear since I was developing breasts. The vest had hook-and-eyes down the center, and did not allow any space for the development of breasts. The chest was flattened.

Together with all the donations of food, staple items, gift and household items which donors and benefactors readily gave, there were other contributions. From the factories all over greater New York came textiles, laces, writing papers, pens and pencils, bolts of fabric, as well as scrap pieces of cloth, leather, plastics, and similar items. These items would be stored in the triple garage on the side of the estate. When enough of these items were accumulated, crates would be filled and shipped to Italy. The Daughters of St Paul had special congressional permission to ship used goods to Rome to assist with the reconstruction and reestablishment of the convents damaged during WW II. It was very clear from the way these crates were packed that Congress did not mean for the nuns to ship any foodstuffs or medicines. However, each crate had its share of food staples and medicine wrapped in cloth and cotton and placed in the center so that if any came under inspection, the inspectors would really have to take the complete contents out of the crate to find the contraband. Each crate weighed from 300 to 500 pounds when filled. There were special pieces of equipment to seal these crates with inch-wide steel strips. There was a scissor-like tool to crimp the strip and thus seal the crate. Twice or three times each year a large truck or semi would back up to the garage and all the crates would be loaded and taken to the docks for shipment to Rome. I do not know if the Order ever paid for this

Throwaway Nun

Rosemary Scirocco-Corsale
Kathleen A. Barreca

shipping and truck service. I recall that Mother Pietra would tell us that the shipment reached Rome and that the Mother General was writing to express her appreciation.

It became very clear that this was an Italian order of nuns, and that there was a fierce, unshakable fidelity to Rome. Mother Pietra had come to the United States in 1932 to establish the Order here. Within eight years, all communication and spiritual direction from the General Motherhouse, the Mother General (*Mother Pietra's superior*), and supports were severed by the outbreak of WW II. Mother Pietra was, therefore, left to her own devices to run the American Province of the Order as she saw fit. It remained mired in old traditions until long after I left. Mother Pietra was the ultimate head of the Daughters of St. Paul in the United States; she ruled with an iron fist, and she freely shipped nuns back to Italy if they became vocal and objected to her rules and regulations. There were some nuns who came to the United States after the war and complained to some of us that the nuns did not work this hard in Italy! They didn't have to; Mother Pietra rode herd over the nuns in the American Province and, in so doing, ingratiated herself more and more to Rome. Rome looked to the U.S. for all their needs, both money and donated items. So, on the shoulders of the nuns in America and through the generosity of the benefactors, Rome was well provided for.

Each religious order of nuns and priests has rules and regulations about their daily activities. They have rules about when to speak and when to be silent,(which is mostly all of the time), they have rules about times of prayer, times of eating, and times of recreation. While in the early years, there were very few occasions of real recreation. I recall that a couple of times after dinner we would jump rope for about 10 or 15 minutes. One of

Throwaway Nun

Rosemary Scirocco-Corsale
Kathleen A. Barreca

the nuns from Italy taught us how to jump double Dutch style. According to the rules of the Order, every nun would be given an hour to one and a half hours of recreation time daily. However, Mother Pietra's attitude was that recreation was just changing work. The only recreation hour left in tack was Thursday evening, this was the time that everyone gathered in the sewing room to darn their black hose, sew articles of clothing needing repair, and to patch large holes. Every day, including Sunday, there would be work to be done; and it was accomplished just as Mother Pietra dictated.

As stated previously, I was a fast learner, spirited, and very willing to please others. I was not afraid of work, and my early eagerness would make me the object of Mother Pietra's assessment of my capabilities. I was placed on this earth, according to her, for manual labor; I was not endowed with intelligence. They were sure to remind me daily by calling me the hurtful names of stupid and retard. There was no reason for them to think about or change their opinions because I never objected. I accepted each negative, and as many as they delivered each day. Hence, they proceeded to treat me as a stupid, unintelligent postulant. No one ever asked how I felt or what I thought. No one cared whether I had any feelings or not. No one every presumed that I was practicing, in blind obedience, the brainwashing.

In the years after WW II, the American Province of the Daughters of St. Paul grew and expanded. There were nuns that came from Italy and stayed in Staten Island until they learned a reasonable command of the English language. Then they were sent to the recently opened convents and media centers. There were also many young girls who entered, some stayed, but most left to return home after a short orientation. After each

Throwaway Nun   Rosemary Scirocco-Corsale
                                                             Kathleen A. Barreca

young girl would leave, we postulants would be lectured and informed that the departure had been because of the girl's lack of generosity, unwillingness to follow the directives of the Mistress or superiors, and that she was throwing away her vocation to religious life, which would certainly call down the wrath of God. Surely, those leaving the convent would become prostitutes, Protestants, and be condemned to hell after death! These admonitions filled me with fear! I was developing scruples and honing my interior selfhood. I had never been told that I had no vocation to religious life and that I had to leave. I was never told that what they perceived in me as stupidity and unintelligence was enough for them to send me back to my parents. On the couple occasions when I was threatened with being sent home, there was never a follow through. From the beginning, we were urged to pray for perseverance; that is, the gift from God to remain in religious life all the days of our lives. And I prayed every day; I prayed especially hard because I was not bright, not gifted, and not worthy for so lofty a calling, or so I was told almost every day.

    As the Order expanded, the Victorian mansion on Staten Island became too small and cramped. In 1950, a much larger estate was purchased in Derby, NY. This small pastoral site was located in Western New York State near Buffalo. On the Lake Erie shore, this 12 acre site contained a large manse with three other houses on the property. The house closest to the front gate was formerly the residence of the groundskeeper and his family. The cottage type house was inhabited by the cooks and kitchen help. The third house was occupied by the chauffeur and his family. There was a greenhouse and an apple orchard with about 12 trees. On the back side of the estate to the left there was a large, round screened patio separated from the manse by a high row of hedges. On the

Throwaway Nun

inside of the patio was a heavy, round picnic table with benches. The breeze from the lake wafted through the patio and made it a very pleasant place to spend time. Also in the rear off to the right was a covered, three-story, wooden staircase descending to the Lake Erie shore. In front of the English cottage there was a large area of grass, which the gardener had sculpted into designs, where various kinds of rose bushes accented the green grass. From the front gate to the manse was the distance of two city-street blocks. The dirt road wound around a small flowerbed which enhanced the main house and made the road look less rough at the main entrance. This estate had formerly belonged to a very influential family which owned prime real estate in Buffalo, NY. The Order, however, had purchased this property from a religious order of priests and brothers. When the nuns took possession of the property in the beginning of the summer of 1950, two priests and a brother remained awaiting the completion of the new construction of their seminary. By late August, they were gone.

It was in early May, 1950, that I was sent home for a brief visit. This was very unusual because the nuns never got vacations and never went home unless one had been on foreign missions; in that case the visits were once every 10 to 15 years. What was strange was that instead of returning to Staten Island, I was ordered to go to Derby. I was the only postulant there among five senior nuns. The only house in use that summer was the manse. I slept in a small room over the kitchen. The senior nuns' rooms were separated by a door closing off the foyer leading to their rooms. Later, I would learn that my bedroom had been used by servants. It was apt because I spent that summer working like a servant girl. I was 16 years old.

Throwaway Nun

Rosemary Scirocco-Corsale
Kathleen A. Barreca

1950 had been declared a "holy year;" that is, a year of special prayer and pilgrimage to Rome. Pilgrims going to Rome would go through "Peter's Door," a portal in the Vatican only opened every 25 years. Those passing through this portal were said to be given special blessings and indulgences. My mother had gone to Italy in 1950 and remained there for five months. During her trip, she visited Rome and the General Motherhouse of the Daughters of St. Paul During her visit with the sisters, she gave them money, yard goods, and foodstuffs. In the meantime back in Ohio, my sisters prepared for their respective weddings. At the same time, the nuns in Youngstown, Ohio made weekly visits to my parents' home. As was then the custom, no one ever locked their doors. Therefore, the nuns could access the inside with ease. During my mother's absence, they helped themselves to almost the entire reserve of home canned tomato sauce, fruits, and vegetables. There were hundreds of jars! The nuns were kind enough to return the empty bottles and leave them on the shelves in the cellar. No member of my family tried to stop them. One of the nuns who unconscionably sapped the hard work my parents put into canning all these jars of sauce and other foodstuffs had the audacity to tell me, much later, that the shelves in my parents' cellar where the jars were reserved were dirty! I said nothing, but I bit my tongue rather than say that their perception of the shelves being dirty did not deter them from cleaning out the store of reserves. This is an example of the generosity of my parents and how they were used by the Order. On those few occasions when they were able to come to Derby to visit, they brought a carload of food. There was once a whole piglet, bushels of green peppers, and tomatoes, dressed chickens, and fruit.

Throwaway Nun

**Rosemary Scirocco-Corsale
Kathleen A. Barreca**

My mother was still in Italy when I was sent home for this unusual visit and then sent to Derby. There were tasks assigned to me every day: wash and dry all dishes after each meal, clean all restrooms, scrub floors, wash windows, sweep porches, help with the laundry, take out the garbage every day, rake and clean flower beds around the manse, vacuum the runners and rug in chapel, and fetch anything that I was told to by the senior nuns. In addition, I was given the job of cleaning and waxing the massive, wood dining room used by the priests. I was kept busy each day. At night, I would be very tired and happy to go to bed. Since I was the only postulant there, I did not eat with the senior nuns. I ate in the kitchen and was served after the nuns had been served. I vividly recall one time when one of the priests came to the back door. He seemed to be shocked to see me eating there alone. He asked, "Why are you eating here?" I remember the stunned look on his face. The abusive treatment of me, however, continued and his observations made no difference. After this incident, I began to pay more attention to what was happening to me. Why was I in Derby alone? Why was I not with the group of postulants in Staten Island? Why was I worked so hard every day? Why was I actually scorned and verbally mistreated by the senior nuns? I felt abandoned, desolate, and depressed. I felt that I was being treated like a servant girl rather than someone aspiring to become a nun. I felt that the nuns wanted me to get so discouraged with my lot that I would beg to be sent home. I thought I had been through the "baptism of fire" during the previous three years to prove the validity of my vocation to religious life. I knew that there had to be suffering and self-denial, but this was more than I had imagined! The remainder of 1950 and 1951 would test my "metal" and change me.

Throwaway Nun

Rosemary Scirocco-Corsale
Kathleen A. Barreca

In August of 1950, 1 was informed that the Motherhouse and apostolate would be moved to Derby the first week of September. Therefore, I was to work extra hard to clean everything, not only in the manse, but in the gatehouse where the postulants and aspirants would be sleeping, and in the cottage which would be used as a schoolhouse. So I came to understand that if I would choose to remain in the convent it meant that I would be used for all manual labor, hard physical work and back-breaking jobs. In a matter of months I would be told that I was not unintelligent and that the Lord had put me on this earth for hard, manual labor! For the remainder of my religious life, I was never made to forget this and was ordered to work accordingly. No one ever asked me how I felt, what I thought, or what my opinion might be. No one ever thought I had a brain or feelings. In early September, 1950, I watched the station wagons roll down the long dirt driveway carrying the nuns and postulants to the new Motherhouse. I was so overjoyed at finally being reunited with my group that I can remember jumping up and down. It seems that during the summer there had been several admissions to postulancy and aspirancy. I did not know these new peers, but we would get to know one another within days.

In late September we started school. The cottage was turned into classrooms and a place for studies. One room housed the teachers. It was at that same time that we got a new Mistress of Postulants. She was Sr. May Alice. She had recently finished her Master's degree from Fordham University in New York City. She also taught history and social studies. Sr. John Mary, in addition to teaching, was assigned to other academic studies like translating texts from Italian to English. Sr. Constance had come from Italy in late 1949. She had come to Derby and was my Italian

Throwaway Nun
Rosemary Scirocco-Corsale
Kathleen A. Barreca

and Latin teacher. During that first year in Derby, I would feel the lash of her unkind words and learn the power she had over the American province because of her closeness with Mother Pietra.

In the rear of the coach house there were four large bays which had housed any number of carriages and automobiles of the previous, wealthy owners. The large doors to each by had been sealed and nailed shut. This would become the apostolate. Various machines for publishing books were installed here. These were a printing press, linotype, trimmer, and stapler, book-back preparer and embossing machines. Each of the postulants was assigned to learn one or more of these machines under the supervision of a senior nun. The supervisor of this printing area, or apostolate, was Sr. Marie Terese. I was assigned to learn the trimmer, a machine which trimmed paperbound books, large sheets, and monthly periodicals. I was taught how to remove and change the 4-foot blade which did all the trimming. Operation of this machine required strength and stamina. I developed both. The book-back preparer was a small, manually operated machine which rounded the sewn backs of books in preparation for hard-cover binding. It took sheer muscle to operate. Once, I accidentally placed my left hand on the front hold bar too far to the left. The large iron bars came crashing down on my small finger, splitting it open. I had to be taken to a local doctor. The finger was so smashed that the only thing the doctor did was place three "butterfly" bandages on it. He also prescribed a powder-like medication to be sprayed on it daily. The finger throbbed and hurt for days after the accident. I was severely reprimanded for being careless and distracted! Over and over again, Sr. Marie Terese would loudly call me the names which tore at my inner being—stupid, distracted, ignorant, and her favorite, "mammalucca." She

Throwaway Nun

**Rosemary Scirocco-Corsale
Kathleen A. Barreca**

seemed to delight in called me these names. None of the other postulants were ever called anything but their given names. In another occasion, I was doing some intricate work on the trimmer and I was holding my middle finger on the paper in order to keep the top pages from curling under. When I turned, the pressure wheel from the iron weights split my nail and the tip of my finger. I was not taken for any medical assistance. One of the nuns washed my finger with peroxide, doused it literally with iodine, and bandaged it. I was back to work on the machine the very next day.

PART TWO

That first year in Derby would prove to be even worse than the three years spent in New York City. Soon after the arrival of my peer group, I was set upon by the new Mistress of Postulants, Sr. Mary Alice and several other nuns. Mother Pietra gave them their orders, obviously, and they obeyed very well. Sr. Marie Terese continued to call me names, and Sr. Constance now began her own vocal protestations of my ignorance, stupidity, and simpleness. During the monthly retreats I began to dread the "passing" because I was subjected to brutal, verbal assaults on almost everything I did. I was not only berated, but a new twist was added: I was informed that I was a very bad example to the other postulants, I was to avoid saying very much to them because I was so ridiculous, and that I had better learn how to bring my whole person under submission and obedience or else lose my vocation. These reprimands not only occurred once a month, but almost daily. Often I was taken aside by Sr. Mary Alice or another senior nun and told to be quiet, modify my senses, walk straighter, keep my feet together when standing, and a host of other such admonitions. I was inwardly crushed each time I was taken to task; each time seemed to be more serious than the previous time. I became deeply depressed. If I did not smile, I was scolded; if I smiled often I was scolded. I became keenly conscious of my precarious situation. At the same time, I was developing such a profound love of my religious vocation. I would have thrown myself down the three and a half story staircase to the Lake Erie shore to save my vocation—to stay in the convent! This burning desire did not go unnoticed, and was used effectively. I knew that I had to

Throwaway Nun

Rosemary Scirocco-Corsale
Kathleen A. Barreca

change, to transform myself, to become a silent, humble, meek, blindly obedient individual with no outward manifestations of opinion, feeling, thought, emotion or word. I had to change the very essence of who I was; I was overwhelmed! Each day the confrontations brought inner turmoil. On each occasion I would lash out at myself in my head, and I began to do as all the others do; denigrate myself. Many years later I would learn that victims, like myself, actually assimilate and function exactly as the perpetrators wish. However, at this time, I neither had the maturity or the coping mechanisms necessary to handle these constant beratings. Over and over again, day after day, I would react inside to the abasements received on the outside. I knew that I could not show any feeling or emotion. I had to learn how to become totally internal; the cost of this was enormous. The depression increased. It began to affect my schoolwork. I still recall during one evening study period when I was given the book, "A Tale of Two Cities," to read for my English class that I read the same page over and over again for more than an hour; I could not comprehend what was written. I turned the pages of that book for many days without remembering the story. To this day, I have never really read this classic. During this time, I began to pray fervently and earnestly during prescribed prayer time which never seemed enough! I found myself praying all of the time. Even in prayer I was self-deprecating. I would plead with my Lord Jesus and His Blessed Mother to forgive me, to grant me perseverance in my vocation, to grant me the graces to change all my evil ways, and to become the person my superiors wanted me to be. Each daily visit to the chapel was drenched with my petitions; each day my prayers became supplications. More and more I drew into myself; more and more I no longer was keenly aware of others in my peer group. I never saw their

Throwaway Nun

Rosemary Scirocco-Corsale
Kathleen A. Barreca

faults or failings; I rarely noticed when they made jest of me. I began to cry myself to sleep each night. To stifle any sob, I would place my pillow over my face. I could find no redeeming qualities in my person; I could find nothing good about myself. I truly believed Mother Pietra and the others who would berate me, agreeing that I really deserved this kind of treatment, and I really deserved to be sent home and to lose my vocation. I felt that I owed homage and deep gratitude to Mother Pietra for allowing me to remain in the convent. Every day, as I awakened to the 5:30 a.m. morning bell, I would dread the day. I wept inwardly every morning because I had to face a new day full of my failures. I could see nothing changing in me, no matter how hard I tried, but I still kept trying....every day, every hour, every waking moment. My tears would lull me to sleep each night. No one ever discovered my nightly shedding of tears. I was becoming very good at hiding my emotions. I was becoming very good at stuffing everything inside.

During this same year I was to continue being treated like a servant girl. Wherever there was heavy and hard work to do, I was assigned to do it. There were over nine acres of lawn. I was taught to operate the tractor mower, and once every two weeks I was sent to mow the lawn. It took the better part of two days to complete. The lawn edges and the lot in front of the cottage had to be cut with a small mower. The long stretch of road leading to the main house had been planted with evergreen trees, and the small mower was used to trim around them, as well. The tractor had a detachable seat. In the beginning I used the seat, but I was told that I would give greater glory to God if I walked and did not sit. So, I never used the seat again! I recall one very hot and humid day in July—even during the early morning hours, the air was stale and heavy—I cut the

Throwaway Nun

**Rosemary Scirocco-Corsale
Kathleen A. Barreca**

grass until I was called for lunch. After lunch, I went back to my task. At no time did anyone call me inside for a break, nor was I given anything to drink. After all, there was no one outside to ask for a drink or a break. I felt the sun burning the top of my head. At 5:30 p.m. I was called to chapel for prayer and to the benediction of the Blessed Sacrament. I had been kneeling just a short time when I felt everything go blank. When I awoke some time later I was lying on the flagstones in front of the back doors. There were several nuns hovering over me, as well as the priest who gave benediction. I remember him saying, "She had sunstroke!" That evening, I was sent with the other postulants to recreation, where Sr. Mary Alice made certain that I was seated and quiet. The next day, I was ordered back out to finish mowing the lawn. Once a month in the heat of summer, I was sent outside to dig the weeds from both sides of the dirt road beginning at the gate to the manse, which was a distance of about two city blocks. An ice hoe was used to scrape the unwelcome weeds which were put into a bushel and dumped on the compost heap at the edge of the wooded area behind the coach house. A rake was then used to smooth the area divested of weeds. My hands would develop large blisters that would break open. They would hurt for days, but I dared not complain; I would be scolded if I did. While I was doing this hard work, everyone else was inside shaded from the sun and either working in the apostolate or studying. I never complained or refused to do any task. After all, I was doing exactly what Mother Pietra and Sr. Constance said....that I had been put on this earth to do manual labor, since I was not endowed with intelligence. Since this was now the Motherhouse and all the printing was done in Derby, shipment of the printed word was made to all of the cities where the convents were located. However, most still was shipped to

Throwaway Nun

Rosemary Scirocco-Corsale
Kathleen A. Barreca

Staten Island. I was there to do the packing and to load the vans and trucks. I was there to do the hard work.

That first winter in Derby was an especially brutal one for everyone. The winds gale off Lake Erie, and as it blew, icy blasts of air came with it. The snows came and stayed. The postulants had black capes with hoods. In the rawness and bitter cold of early morning, we would line up, two by two, and walk from the gatehouse where we slept to the manse where the chapel was located. We looked like a line of Little Black Riding Hoods! The talk amongst the postulants, out of earshot of the superiors, was that no one really liked these capes. They were not warm enough, and no one wanted to look like a storybook character! There was never a change of clothing made. The cape and hood were the only things that poorly protected the growing body from the bitter, winter cold and snow. Once in the manse, I was to proceed to the cellar and shovel the coal into the furnace. When I was finished with that task, I was to shovel the ashes, put them in large, handled cans which I would place outside for garbage collection once weekly. Only the manse had a coal furnace. The gatehouse, the cottage and coach house had gas heat.

All during my religious life my parents provided me with shoes and winter galoshes. In those years the plastic was thick and hard and the pair I had fit over my shoes. Also, the winters were much bitterer than they are today. It was not unusual to get 2 or 3 feet of snow from evening to morning. So, I was in the main house doing my extra chores. My peer group had already left for school and study period. My boots were in the small entryway to the kitchen where everyone entered the manse who was not a visitor. Sr. Evangelista was in the kitchen preparing for dinner. She heard me let out a big "sigh" and immediately came to the entryway to see

Throwaway Nun

**Rosemary Scirocco-Corsale
Kathleen A. Barreca**

what had happened. When I had tried to put my left shoe into the boot, the back tore from under the top to the heel. I immediately consigned myself to telling a senior nun and admitting my fault in the matter. Sister Evangelista did not wait to tell me how careless I was and how inconsiderate. The inclement weather might cause me to catch a cold without boots. If this were to happen, I would not be able to do all my chores and tasks. I told her that I would write to my parents and get some new boots as soon as we were permitted to write letters, which was only on Sunday evenings. The next day as I was leaving out the back door for school, Sister Evangelista stopped me and pointed to a pair of galoshes and told me that they were mine. She said that she had gotten a pair for herself as well. I was dumbfounded. I said nothing. The black galoshes were a man's size 10 and the ones worn over the shoes with the metal hasps and zipper from the top to the middle of the arch. At the time, I wore a size 9 shoe. The galoshes were a few sizes too big and created many walking hazards. The tips would get caught between the paving stones on the path to the cottage where we slept. I would trip going to the schoolhouse. I would trip anywhere and everywhere. Once when I was in the city, the senior nun and I were waiting for the bus to return to the convent. I caught a glimpse of myself in a department store window. I looked hideous and deformed. My galoshes made my feet look like those of a circus clown. I was humiliated, but could say nothing. I kept my silence. Wearing these atrocious galoshes lasted until I left for New York in 1952. I left the boots in Derby, and dreaded the thought they might actually send them to New York, but I never received them much to my comfort. My parents did send me an overshoe type of short boot. Later I would recognize them as "Totes." This experience was sufficiently

Throwaway Nun

Rosemary Scirocco-Corsale
Kathleen A. Barreca

traumatic to the degree that I have not worn any form of boots or overshoes since I left the convent.

The idiosyncrasies and deficits of this estate began to demonstrate their ugly heads that winter. Since the lake froze, there was no water source. Whenever water did succeed in coming from the taps, it was collected in pails, pots, and bottles. This was reserved for cooking. We were permitted to bathe once a week and then with very little water. Often the weekly bath was more of a "sponge bath." During the winter, we did not wash our hair; we were not permitted to wash our hair until spring. Rather, we were given fine-tooth combs to use every day. There were those who had serious dandruff problems, and they found it very difficult not to be able to wash their hair. I was glad that I did not have the problem.

Because of the lack of water, the water that was used to cook the spaghetti was later used to wash the dishes. We ate some form of pasta twice weekly. On the other days, we would use leftover water from the various containers. There were several large "chuckholes" on the property, and when it rained, water would accumulate in these depressions. The postulants would line up with pails to collect this water, which was then dumped into the bathtub and later used for flushing the toilets. *(No one was permitted to flush after each individual use; upon orders from the senior nun or teacher, we would take turns going to the bathroom and when the last person finished, she flushed the toilet. then, a pail of water would be taken from the bathtub to fill the tank.)*

It was in the spring of 1951 that Mother Pietra began to take steps to resolve the water problem. It was the first time that I had ever seen a dowser and I was fascinated. The dowsing rod turned straight down between two large trees alongside of the manse. The next day, large equipment was delivered to the site. An artesian well had been tapped, and the contractors would put in a tap line and faucet from the well into the cellar. Every lunch and dinnertime, it was my task to get the well water in gallon jugs for drinking. This well helped to solve some of the water problems, but during the winter, there was a continued water shortage which everyone adjusted to. My days and nights continued to be filled with depression, denigration, and self-abasement. It was so difficult for me to keep my mind on my schoolwork, and I would often spend study time praying. I know I did not do well in my classes or with my homework. I was so confused and inwardly distraught that I doubled my prayers in an effort to change the very nature of whom I was in order to persevere in my religious vocation. Since the postulants and aspirants were in school during weekdays, every recreation time was spent in the apostolate. At this time, there were a number of new admissions to the convent who were not of Italian descent.

Many simple adjustments were made in order to be accommodating. Butter was now put on the table for every meal, more meat and potatoes were presented at mealtime, there were more meal variations, and breakfast saw more toast. It was the first time since my admission that everyone spoke English during the day; it was the first time that conferences and retreats were in English. Italian was now the second language.

On more than one occasion, I would be called out of a study period to do manual work, like pack boxes for shipping, stack materials, move furniture or equipment, or to set up the work for the others when they would come into the apostolate. When the postulant's dormitory had been

Throwaway Nun

**Rosemary Scirocco-Corsale
Kathleen A. Barreca**

changed to the coach house, more than once I was awakened by the Mistress of Postulants at midnight. I would dress and go downstairs to the apostolate. I would work at the trimming machine until the others awoke to the bell at 5:30 a.m. I would then go upstairs to wash my face and hands, brush my teeth, and comb my hair before leaving with the others for chapel in the manse. I was expected to do all the usual study and/or work for the remainder of that day. I did not mind these physically exhausting days and nights. When I did get into bed, I was so spent that I would fall to sleep immediately without the crying.

    The postulants would take turns washing the dishes after each meal. With the water shortage, the task became a science. Strained water from washing and cooking vegetables was saved for the "first wash;" that is, cleaning most of what was on the plate. The second pan of water was heated and soapy. This was the final wash water. The rinse water came from various containers. Others would dry and put the dishes away. One day, I was at the sink washing dishes. I felt a pair of hands around my ankles. Sister Constance had tied my feet together with a rope. I was dumbfounded as were the others in the kitchen. Not a word was said. She smiled and left the room. When she had gone, I bent down to untie the rope and I threw it in the garbage. No one ever spoke a word; no one had ever told her that I had untied my feet and threw away the rope. Contrary to what I had expected, Sr. Constance never brought up the subject; neither did anyone else. I already described how poorly and devastated I felt and how ungainly I performed. It would be my fate to have broken three dishes during the course of several months. On the last occasion, Sr. Constance was in the kitchen, which made me even more nervous and clumsy. When the dish crashed to the floor, she berated me and said that I

Throwaway Nun

**Rosemary Scirocco-Corsale
Kathleen A. Barreca**

would have to write a letter home to my parents and request that they send money to Mother Pietra for new dishes. I trembled inside; I had been through this before when my father's reply provided fuel for many humiliations and scolding's. However, I was never ordered to write the letter and I was very grateful. After this incident, I was extra careful and never broke a dish again for a very long time!

Before or immediately after Easter, some nuns returned to the convent from the city where they were either selling books or gathering donated food. Whichever their mission they came back with a duckling. It was placed in the greenhouse. The next day I was ordered to feed it and change the water. So, after breakfast, I would be given just one slice of bread. On a few occasions I was given a basket of outer leaves from cauliflower and cabbage to feed to the growing duck. However, the duck never ate a single piece of these greens. At times I would ask for more bread because one slice a day was just not enough. I was told that if the duck refused to eat the leaves then he was not hungry and did not need any more bread. On occasion I would be able to put some crusts or even a half slice of bread in my pocket to feed the starving bird. Although I was prohibited from spending much time in the greenhouse with him, I remember the way he looked at me. His eyes were soulful and sad. It broke my heart to have to go into the greenhouse every day with this meager bread. As the spring passed and summer set about, the greenhouse got very hot. I asked if I could put a tub of some kind in the greenhouse so that the duck could refresh himself from the heat, however, my request was denied. In early October my peer group and I went to the main house for lunch. Each of us had a very small piece of meat on our plates. Mother Pietra announced that this was "duck" and that it was very tasty. I had not been told that they were contemplating killing the duck and eating it. One of the postulants let out a small scream and pushed her chair away from the table, vowing that she would never eat "our pet duck." In all the months the duck was in the greenhouse, no one ever stopped by or took food there. No one but I saw the duck every day. When I heard it was the duck we were eating, I was greatly relieved. The duck was out of its misery and I was no longer to see him suffer. It would be many years later that I would come to believe that one can judge how another human being treats his fellow humans by the way they treat animals. A short time later, that postulant would leave the convent for good.

Sometime during that first year in Derby, Mother Pietra sent a cover letter and an invoice to each of the postulants' parents. She explained that the Order was paying a great deal of money to keep and educate their beloved daughters. Hence, the $365 requested for room and board was a small pittance, and payment would show goodwill and resolution to support the religious vocation of their child. My parents paid the sum (one needs to realize that in 1950-51 $365 was a small fortune to a family of average income). My family did not know that I more than paid for my keep with all the tasks, manual labor, and midnight awakenings to work in the apostolate, and grounds keeping. They never learned about the sunstroke, all of the blisters on my hands, nor all the calluses on my knees. This was the first and only time such a letter was sent; Mother Pietra was in a quandary to raise money, and billing the parents of the American postulants was her solution. It proved not to be as successful as she thought!

There were those occasions when I was allowed recreation time with the other postulants. On one balmy day, we were playing some sort

Throwaway Nun

Rosemary Scirocco-Corsale
Kathleen A. Barreca

of catch ball. I was running backwards and slipped into the small decline that marked the base of the hedges surrounding the schoolhouse. I sprained my ankle. The next morning after breakfast I told Sr. Mary Alice. She told me to wait downstairs while she went upstairs to ask Mother Pietra what to do. I waited at the bottom of the staircase and I could hear every word. After Sr. Mary Alice reported the problem with my ankle, Mother Pietra stated that she did not believe me, that I was trying to get attention, that I was trying to avoid more work, and that my complaint did not deserve any further concern. She told Sr. Mary Alice to allow me to soak my foot and ankle in a pan of salted water. I can still remember the "put out" look on Sr. Mary Alice's face as she gave me the pan and salt. I can still remember the tone of voice used by Mother Pietra. For the next week I really struggled to bear weight on that foot; it took several weeks before the swelling abated. At no time did anyone ask to see my injury. I dared not grimace in pain lest I should be scolded. On another occasion when we were at play, I accidentally bumped another postulant. Sr. Mary Alice gave me a hard, backhanded blow across my face. I was so stunned, I just stood still, our eyes locked for a couple of seconds and then she turned away. The next day during the evening study period, Sr. Mary Alice sat at the desk in front of the classroom and was crying. She held a handkerchief in her hand and her face was red. She told the group that there are times when a nun does not give good example, and if she had done anything to show poor judgment to the group, she was sorry. While relating this, she averted my eyes. I knew that she had been instructed not to apologize to me specifically, but to the entire group. After this confession, no one ever made mention of the incident again.

Throwaway Nun   Rosemary Scirocco-Corsale
                                                                                  Kathleen A. Barreca

      The word "abuse" was not in my vocabulary. In those years, abuse was very rarely used to describe treatment of individuals. Since then, I have learned the word, its ramifications, and its meanings. I know now that I was physically, emotionally, and mentally abused. In the 1950's, I did not know that the United States had child labor laws. I know now that the Order violated those laws. How incomprehensible is the fact that this vicious abuse and violation of person and dignity was campaigned in the name of Jesus! How incomprehensible is the fact that this abuse and vicious violation of person and the Child Labor Laws of the United States was perpetrated by a group of people who professed to live the lives of angels and were consecrated to Jesus!

      And, so passed every painful day; every sorrowful week; and every devastating month; of that first year in Derby. It was in spring of 1951 that I began to feel a change in myself. I was less talkative, less "visible," more obedient, more submissive, and more compliant. I was becoming an expert at hiding all my emotions and feelings; my face was becoming blank— never baring my soul to anyone. I was becoming very good at internalizing all the abuse, all the negatives, and at keeping everything inside. I was finally beginning to become a very different person, to control my very nature, and to comply with the desires of my superiors. I had to keep pretending that I was stupid and ignorant, and that I was aware of nothing. Nothing and no one was aware of me. Every day I struggled to keep the essence of myself under control. I clearly understood that I could never be the exuberant, intelligent person I really was. I struggled every day to fit into the mold which Mother Pietra, Sr. Constance, and the selected senior nuns had set for me. Every day, I was getting better and better at squeezing into that mold. Inside myself I felt I was succeeding in

Throwaway Nun Rosemary Scirocco-Corsale
Kathleen A. Barreca

my endeavor to be a different person. I could never share with anyone—neither my peers nor superiors. If they saw changes, they never told me. If I was becoming more submissive and compliant, they never said anything to me. If I was fitting into the mold they set for me, they never encouraged my efforts. The warm and gentle breezes of spring were chasing the coldness and icy blasts wafting off Lake Erie. But with spring came a lifting of the darkness that had pervaded my every waking moment for the past year or more. I was still depressed and I was still a scapegoat. However, I felt that I was halfway out of a deep hole. I seemed increasingly better able to buffer the abuses. I was not reacting to the unkind names; I was absorbing my lot like a dry sponge. I began to accept my inner pains and emotional upheaval as the conditions for the perseverance of my religious life. I came to this springtime aware that I had developed a very special kind of prayer life. Though I had been in the convent for four years, I had never been taught about a personal relationship with my Lord, a rebirth in the Holy Spirit, or centered or contemplative prayer. My superiors had been so busy monitoring and berating me for all the temporal things, they neglected the guidance and support in my spiritual journey. In this area I had been left alone, and with God I could be the person I was; He didn't seem to mind my lack of sophistication, my zest for life and living. Since I could not show the essence of myself outwardly, I began an unending dialogue with Jesus and His Blessed Mother. Prayer was my only solace in the midst of the tempests raging around me. It would remain my bulwark for the remainder of my religious life.

    To this day, I do not know where I got the stamina to endure the abuse heaped upon me. I do not know where I got the courage to continue

Throwaway Nun

Rosemary Scirocco-Corsale
Kathleen A. Barreca

in this negative environment every day. I do not know how I did not become suicidal with the degree of depression I suffered. I will never understand what preserved my mental health. If there is anything to prove the power of prayer, it might well be my life in the convent. No one, physically or mentally, could have sustained this personal devastation without some mental or physical manifestation of the abuse.

As the days got warmer, I became keenly aware of everything surrounding me. It seemed like I could see every bud on every tree, bush, and stalk. I heard every song the birds had to sing. The skylark has a very unusual song; it has only two notes of a very sad whistle. I heard it every day. Twenty-three years before, songstress Roberta Flack recorded the song, "Killing Me Softly with His Song," I felt a kinship with that soulful whistle. As I listened to the skylark, I felt the strings of my heart plucked. I, too, felt like I was dying inside. The sad whistle sang my song. Even today, I am still moved by the skylark. There was a large tree growing at the edge of the road near the manse. Every day I watched the buds develop into small leaves, which I then watched grow big and wide covering the branches and spreading shade in their wake. This tree began to be a symbol for me; there was a time for each season, and with it, transformation and change. It appeared to me that the tree would painfully go through these changes; the end result was extraordinary beauty. In spring, the buds would burst into a magnificent green coat and give shelter to many birds. In the fall, the colors would be dazzling before the leaves would die and fall to the ground. Then, every branch and every twig would lend itself to holding the snows and ice of winter. I thought that this tree symbolized my life in the convent; after each season of pain and anguish, I would be transformed and changed. I loved that tree; it is still there!

I was very concerned about my final exams. I knew that I had not done well in my studies the past year. Algebra was my worst subject. I trembled to think of what would happen to me if I did not get promoted to my senior year of high school. Would I be sent home? Would I lose my vocation? Would I be the one to disgrace my family by being sent home for failure to succeed in high school? This inner turmoil grew as exam time drew near. I expressed my concern to Sr. Nazareth, who assured me that I would do well. Do well? Did she know something that I did not know? As one of my teachers, she was aware that I had not done well during the past year. However, I never mentioned the matter again. The study periods became very intense for me; I tried hard to concentrate on the reviews of my academic subjects, so that I could be as ready as possible for the exams. I prayed that I would not be called out of my study times for work in the apostolate or some other manual labor, for I had been subject to these orders often during the last year. When grades had been passed out after the exams, I was relieved to see that I scored in the 90's in every subject, except algebra. In this subject I scored in the mid-80's, and I was promoted to grade 12. I was elated but I had learned not to show any emotion. Even having received those scores I still believed that I was unintelligent and stupid. If my teachers perceived that I had any intelligence, they never stated so. If they believed that I had any talent, they never pointed the way and never supported any endeavor on my behalf. I was still thought of as a simpleton and was treated as such!

The summer of 1951 saw several postulants leave the convent and several others enter, including a 21-year-old young lady who had left her

Throwaway Nun

**Rosemary Scirocco-Corsale
Kathleen A. Barreca**

home in the middle of the night because her parents had objected so vociferously to her religious vocation. Since there was no summer school, daytime was spent in the apostolate operating the various machines and doing all the work needed for the paper and the hardcover binding of books. With all these hands, the linotyping, printing, and embossing machines were operating at capacity, often in shifts and into the nights. Often I was ordered to go to work at the trimming machine after dinner. Most often, Sr. David from Brazil or Sr. Camille from Italy would be at the printing press. I knew from experience that these two nuns were not Mother Pietra's spies; I knew that they were very kind and that I had nothing to fear. I think that I was born with a very good soprano voice. From my youth, I could sing high notes, and I loved to sing. However, soon after my entrance into religious life, I was being reproached for singing too loudly, being heard above the others, and accused for acting as though I was the only person in the convent who could sing. Consequently, I learned to sing softly and to blend my voice with the others. Those evenings spent workings at the trimmer in the apostolate was my singing time . . . and sing I did! One of my favorite hymns was and is the "Ave Maria." I sang unrestrained! On more than one occasion, the sisters turned off the printing press to hear me sing. They would ask me to repeat the hymn. Sr. Camille could not seem to get enough of the "Ave Maria." One evening she came to stand by the trimming machine. When I had finished singing she took my hand, and with tears in her eyes, said, "Don't ever stop singing." Shortly after this wonderful incident, she returned to Italy, never knowing that I could not sing like that when other nuns were present. In fact, the following winter we were learning to sing the "Mass of St. Lucy," a complex musical piece written for a four-voice

Throwaway Nun

**Rosemary Scirocco-Corsale
Kathleen A. Barreca**

harmony. Sr. Nazareth was the organist and we would practice for at least one hour every evening after dinner. There was a section of the "Gloria" that required a strong soprano voice that could reach past high C. I was the only one who could sustain singing that high. So, Sr. Nazareth gave me this 12-bar solo to sing. We practiced in preparation for Christmas, when we would sing this wonderful Mass. We sounded so good in practice. In early December, Mother Pietra who had a very deep voice in the baritone range returned from one of her many trips to the various convents. She had learned the bass harmony of this Mass in Italy. No one had such a deep voice like hers. That night we gathered to practice and she was with the group. In the middle of my solo, she ordered me to stop singing and Sr. Nazareth to stop playing the organ. She demanded to know why I had been given this solo. Sr. Nazareth explained that the notes were so high in these few bars and that I was the only one who could sing them without difficulty. Mother Pietra ruled that there would be no solo and that everyone would sing to the best of their abilities through the high notes. She never canceled her own solos. So, the group sang the high notes and I was sure not to be heard above them.

During the summer of 1951, the postulants were permitted to go out with the senior nuns to sell books and seek donations. When Sr. Marie Terese told my Superiors that I could be spared from the apostolate, I, too, would be allowed to go into the greater Buffalo area to sell religious books and pamphlets. The trip into Buffalo was made on the Greyhound bus and took approximately 45 minutes to reach the big city from Derby. I enjoyed these trips. I enjoyed the ride along Route 20 which was just south of the lake. There are many large estates along the way, and each home had its own unique landscaping. In the spring and summer, the yards sported

Throwaway Nun

Rosemary Scirocco-Corsale
Kathleen A. Barreca

flowers of every description with a palette of colors. I enjoyed spending the better part of the day away from the demands of my emotion and my muscle. What I perceived on these trips into Buffalo and the surrounding areas was that the people were very different from those living in the greater New York City area. They lived a slower and simpler lifestyle. Most had their own homes and no one lived in tenements like they did in New York. The distinctive accent that was so common in the eastern half of New York State didn't exist in this area. People seemed more willing to take time. It seemed to me that the majority of the Roman Catholic population in greater Buffalo was of Polish descent. They were very devout and gave us great respect. No matter where I went, the houses were well maintained. The lawns were manicured and each house had some form of landscaping. Some had bushes, while others had both bushes and flowers. I saw no ghettos or areas where the houses were not well cared for. What I was most impressed with was the neatness and cleanliness of the inside of these residences. It did not matter if the furnishings were old or new, fancy or plain, ornate or simple, costly or cheap. There seemed to be a great pride in the maintenance of the home, inside and out. One could, proverbially, eat off the floors in almost every home.

To the west of the convent lies Derby-On-The-Lake and during the summer, scores of people would descend upon this small hamlet to bask on the sandy beach. Many owned cottages while the greater number of families rented or stayed with relatives who owned property there. It was a favorite spot to sell books during the summer. At the end of the day, the senior nun would ask a kind person for a ride back to the convent. I remember on one such return the driver of this large, red convertible was a young man. He had been requested to drive the "good sisters" back to the convent. He wore sandals, an old pair of trousers, and was bare chested. The top of the convertible was down. The young man drove so fast that I could hardly catch my breath. I was hanging on to my lace veil and I saw the senior sister do the same. That five-mile trip was made in record time!

During those first two years in Derby, the group of postulants, accompanied by the Mistress and a teacher, was taken to visit the renowned Basilica of Our Lady of Victory in Lackawanna, New York. We toured the Basilica, knelt to pray, visited the orphanage, and ate the lunches we carried with us in the dining room of the building next to the church. On another occasion, we were taken to visit Niagara Falls, New York. We were taken to the overhang which allowed us to look straight down into the Falls on the American side. We listened to the roar of the falling water and watched the foam where the water fell among the boulders. Years later, this very overhang would break loose and fall, causing the death of several visitors. We did not go into the caves behind the Falls, nor did we ride the boat that sails under the Falls. Years later, I would have many occasions to visit Niagara Falls, both on the American and Canadian sides. I cannot recall very many other educational or religious outings; this kind of learning, seeing, and recreation was considered a treat, and a rare one, at that!

In early September, 1951, I began my senior year of high school. From the beginning it became apparent to me that I would not have the difficulties of the last year. I was able to study, to concentrate, and to retain for better comprehension. This does not mean that the scapegoating had ceased; I had learned a great deal about enduring the abuse and hiding feelings and emotions. This last year of school was void of my dreaded subject—algebra. I did not take geometry or calculus. However, I found

Throwaway Nun

**Rosemary Scirocco-Corsale
Kathleen A. Barreca**

myself enjoying school, enjoying studying, and I enjoyed doing my homework. I loved my English assignments, and I wanted to devour as much reading as possible. However, I was permitted to read only so much. I recall being given a volume of prose, short stories, and poetry. I had been assigned to read a short story entitled, The King's English.-unbeknownst to anyone, I read most of the book. To this day I can remember the poem, "Sonnet by an Indian Girl;" the words seemed to say what was in my soul. It spoke about the escape of the soul through myriads of rules and regulations that kept people fettered to their environs. I, too, wanted to escape these four walls and fly through space under blue skies. I wanted to fly away every day from the pain and the agony of the trials to which I was subjected. Like the Indian girl in the poem, I saw the beauty of the blue skies and the azure seas. Like her, I, too, heard the "evening bells of Arcady." In retrospect, it was my God-given ability to escape to these places of beauty that kept my mind intact. Other than the Tale of Two Cities I never read the classics or modern literature. Though the Daughters of St. Paul were missionaries of the modern media and printed books, magazines, pamphlets, tracts, and leaflets, we were never allowed to read anything without permission. At best, I had been given the stories about two nuns of the Order who had lived exemplary lives and who had died very prematurely in Italy. When the nuns printed, collated, and bound the Holy Bible, we were forbidden to read any of it. When the four Gospels and the Epistles had been completed as two separate, soft-cover books, we were each given a copy. I still have those given to me that many years ago. It would be long after my convent exit that I would read the Bible. Notwithstanding this lack of "rounding" of my education, I continued to do well in my senior year. In fact, I did so well that I had completed all of

Throwaway Nun

Rosemary Scirocco-Corsale
Kathleen A. Barreca

the subjects and texts by December. I had completed high school and I was 16 years old. I was unsure, exactly, what my superiors would order of me. I knew that I would never be sent to college because I was considered to have little or no intelligence even though I completed school early and my having done well on exams. Not my teachers, peers, nor Mother Pietra said anything. After all, no one deliberately incurred her displeasure. To do so would be to suffer the rainfall of her wrath, the scourge of her anger, and the whip of her verbal abuses. They were much smarter than I.

In late June, 1952, just after we had said prayers before lunch, Mother Pietra called my name. I was surprised and was trembling inside as I walked to the rear of the senior nuns' table where she presided. She handed me a small, manila envelope with the name "Postulant Rosemary" scribbled across the front partially covering the address. She said nothing else. When I returned to my seat, I opened the envelope and removed the contents. It was my high school diploma from Mother Cabrini Academy in Fort Washington, New York. No one ever said a word. I returned the diploma to the envelope. Acknowledgment of the completion of my high school studies was never given to me by Mother Pietra, none of my teachers, senior nuns, or members of my peer group. No one congratulated me, even cursorily, or made any other gesture which may have verified my person as a high school graduate. Inwardly, I was hurt, even though I had come to learn to accept this rejection and being a nonentity. I was then informed that I could write home to let my family know that I had gotten my diploma. My family responded immediately with greeting cards, and their letters were filled with approval. My parents also sent me a gift of $20, but I was never given the money. It was removed from the envelope before being given to me. The very next year, four of my co-postulants

Throwaway Nun

Rosemary Scirocco-Corsale
Kathleen A. Barreca

graduated from high school. A big dinner was held with a formal presentation of diplomas and special recognitions. A decorated cake and ice cream capped off the sumptuous meal. After dinner the entire community gathered in the room off the main foyer to continue the festivities. The graduates were seated or stood next to Mother Pietra. I had occasion to stop in front of her to receive her sign of the Cross and tapping on my forehead. While she did this, I looked directly in her eyes, but, as usual, she averted my stare. At the time of this occurrence, I was not mature and sophisticated enough to read body language. Her averting of eyes spoke more than a thousand words. She was having her own scruples about the abuse and suffering which she and her favorite spies caused me, but she never relented.

It was the custom for a postulant to receive the "habit of the Order" after finishing high school. It was June, yet no one talked about my vestition. I had learned from experience not to bring up these kinds of subjects. I waited with anticipation, but my wait was in vain. Every year the entire community would go into a one-week retreat which was called the "spiritual exercises," after which the postulants would receive their habits and the novices would make their "profession of vows." During this retreat, I had my usual conference with Mother Pietra and received the usual put-downs and reprimands. No mention was ever made of vestition; no mention was made that I would be sent home, either. The task of informing me of the bad news fell to Sr. Marie Terese, supervisor of the apostolate. Often she and I would be working alone together, because the senior nuns would be out selling books and the postulants still would be in school. Little by little she began to tell me the process by which I had been denied receiving the habit that year. It appeared that Mother Pietra had

Throwaway Nun
Rosemary Scirocco-Corsale
Kathleen A. Barreca

"consulted" with the senior nuns. (*Always shrewdly, she would absolve herself by referring to the general or unanimous "consensus of the community", having all the nuns agree with her wishes. Since she ruled with an iron fist, no one ever dared to disagree with her*!) Hence, Sr. Marie Terese told me that I was considered too immature and not ready to wear the habit. I was heartbroken; I was devastated! What had I done wrong? Where had I gone wrong? What had I missed? I had suffered the abuses, becoming a very submissive, obedient, pliable individual. I talked little, worked hard, and learned to subdue the very essence of myself to become the kind of person my superiors wanted. I learned to shove everything internally. Rarely, did the exuberant Rosemary raise her head; the denial crushed my entire being! It nullified the transformation I had worked on with so much suffering. For many months I mulled over these questions. I wept each night even longer and harder. I dared not share these questions and concerns with anyone because I had learned from experience to trust no one, to share with no one, or to discuss anything about myself, because that would be certain to make matters worse. Again, I prayed fervently, but not for the grace of being allowed to receive the habit. I prayed for the courage and strength to endure this new assault. I prayed that I would be able to be more of a changed person; I prayed that I would be given the stamina to break out of the "hold of depression." And so, I waited!

Throwaway Nun   **Rosemary Scirocco-Corsale**
                                                                                                     Kathleen A. Barreca

PART THREE

Soon after I had entered the convent back in 1947, I learned that postulants were to write letters addressed to Mother Pietra on holidays, feast days, and on her birthday. These were to be read aloud to the community following the main meal while we were eating dessert. The senior nuns would compose lyrics using the melodies of songs they knew before their convent life, or those learned in Italy, Once; they even used an aria from an opera. The contents of the letter, while mentioning the Divine Master, the Blessed Mother, and any one of the Saints, was replete with the glowing praises of Mother Pietra. Both the letters and songs rendered adulation and glory to her; they detailed her accomplishments and sanctified her virtues. Her praises, extolled in that manner, never let you forget that she was in charge of the Order in the United States, and that she was to be rendered the appropriate homage. Therefore, whenever she was greeted, she would put out her hand to be kissed. Whenever she returned from any of her trips, even just overnight, her hand would be kissed. It was always a mystery to me why her hands were so large, and why the backs of them were so hairy. I have seen some senior nuns who wanted to incur greater favoritism from Mother Pietra actually grab both of her hands and kiss them over and over again! I have seen the broad smiles run across her face during these occurrences. These kinds of adulation and accolades never seemed to make her tire of them; she never seemed embarrassed or tried to stop such glorification. Whenever the Mother General from Italy visited the United States, she was keenly aware of how Mother Pietra was treated. She was very alert to the special manner in which she was treated, but never put a stop to it. After all, to try to abate

Throwaway Nun

**Rosemary Scirocco-Corsale
Kathleen A. Barreca**

this kind of veneration of Mother Pietra would be too serious and stop the general flow of money and goods from the United States to Rome!

It was on just such a religious feast day in 1952 that we were all writing letters to Mother Pietra. As an added feature to my letter, I drew a picture of the Divine Master and colored it with artists' pencils. The original is a very famous painting by a Renaissance artist and hangs in the Vatican. I copied from a holy card that I had in my possession at that time. (I still have that card.) I used it as a cover for the letter. After reading my letter, I handed it to her as was customary. She looked at the drawing. There was no mistaking that she was impressed and liked it. However, she never said a word to me. After a few days, Sr. John Mary called me out of study period. She handed me a small book and told me to read it. It was a primer on art in which the author wrote about perspectives, contrasts, light and dark, shadowing, and charcoal sketching. About a week later I returned the book to Sr. John Mary. She told me to keep the book and study it from cover to cover. I read and reread this book. After a month or so, I informed Sr. John Mary that I had finished studying the book. She then stated that I was to design a cover for the new book that the Order was printing about the life of Saint Imelda. I was taken aback! I looked straight into her face, but I did not detect any misgivings. I returned to my study period in a state of quandary and anxiety. What did I know about art? Because I had the natural ability to draw well did not make me a trained, knowledgeable artist. I knew nothing about the human form, composition, brushes and brush strokes, or various kinds of paints. I had never taken a class in art. All I had done was read one small book about art. I trembled inside. I agonized over this matter for a few weeks. I was never given anytime to do this artwork; I was not given any materials with

Throwaway Nun

**Rosemary Scirocco-Corsale
Kathleen A. Barreca**

which to work. So, over the period of those weeks, I suffered through my feeble attempts to create this extraordinary book jacket. All I used was a single pencil and plain paper. I threw several pieces of paper out. I had to ask permission to use each piece of paper, and again permission to throw any away. Sr. Mary Alice, our Mistress of Postulants and study-period monitor, never objected. She knew that I had been told to do this project. I tried and tried, I drew and drew; I erased and erased. I had the idea and the composition correct, but I simply could not produce the kind of professional quality drawing they expected of me. My drawing of the kneeling figure was boxy and the facial features were primitive. Nonetheless, when I was sure that I had done the best I could do, I presented my paper drawing to Sr. John Mary. She looked at it, returned it to me, and very simply said, "No." After this, nothing more was said of my artwork; nothing more was ever mentioned of my talent. I felt very badly. Here I was, again proving that I was stupid and unintelligent. It would take weeks before I came to realize what had happened. I had natural talent for art; there was no question about that. Even with such natural talent, one must have the proper training, the schooling and the experiences of drawing, painting, use of brushes, and all the myriad things people learn in art school. My talent was being sabotaged; I would never be sent to art school. If I could not be that experienced, professional, exceptional artist at age 16, then I deserved the various names that I was called. And so my talent was disregarded and I continued to be treated as a simpleton.

Within one year, the postulants would make up an anniversary book to be presented to Mother Pietra. I drew and painted all the borders on the pages, some being very intricate. I drew and colored the wreath

Throwaway Nun

**Rosemary Scirocco-Corsale
Kathleen A. Barreca**

around her picture. Because my days were filled with studies and working at the trimming machine, there were times that I was given permission to stay up for an hour or two after bedtime so that I could draw, color, and paint. After dinner when the book had been presented to Mother Pietra, she asked who had done the artwork. When she was told that it was me, she looked through the book and never mentioned a word about my work. She did, however, express how well put together the book was. Her failure and avoidance to mention anything about the art was noticed by more than one postulant. They talked to me about it the next day, and I shrugged off the affront. Nothing was ever mentioned again. It was no surprise to me that my talent was never supported, praised, advanced, or furthered. Like my natural talent for voice and music, these would be left to dry up within me. I was not worth putting any effort into; I was not worth any consideration. I was expendable; the only thing that I was good for was manual and hard labor.

In those years, the machines for printing and bookbinding in the apostolate were almost state of the art. After the pages of a manuscript were given to the linotypist, lines of lead would fall onto a tray. These would be placed on a larger tray and the type was secured. A roller dipped in printer's ink was run over the type followed by a long, narrow paper. A large manually operated roller would be pressed over this and the pages of a book would be printed. These were called "gallies," and each word and line had to be proofread by someone reviewing the original manuscript. Then, printer's marks would be placed on the gallies and returned for corrections. When the corrections had been made, a second gaily was proofread.

Throwaway Nun

Rosemary Scirocco-Corsale
Kathleen A. Barreca

When all corrections had been completed, this type would be mounted on special frames to be printed into the pages of the book. One day, I was called out of the apostolate by Sr. Nazareth to read gallies. She took me to the schoolhouse and we sat in the study room. I read the original manuscript and she held the gallies. We were at this job for just over an hour when Sr. Constance became irate and perturbed. In no uncertain terms she told Sr. Nazareth that I was not intelligent enough to do the reading, and I was never to do that job again! She ordered me back to the apostolate to do the heavy work. I am sure she told Sr. Nazareth a thing or two after I left; I never would be called upon or asked to do any intelligent task again.

In that summer of 1951, an unusual thing happened. The entire community of nuns was informed that a seamstress would be sewing bathing suits for us, and that we would be permitted to go swimming in Lake Erie. This was such a treat and everyone rejoiced! During the sweltering summers this would be a chance to bathe more than once a week, as well as being very refreshing! The bathing suits were light blue and aqua. They were made of a waterproof, canvas fabric. There was a large shirt with below-the-elbow length sleeves and hung down below the knees. The neck was rounded and was closed at the neck with a large snap. Under the shirt was a large "bloomer" with an elastic waist. The boy-type legs also came below the knees. The waterproof material and the clumsiness of the suit prevented true swimming. Dog paddling, wading, and floating were the best that anyone could do. Outside earshot of the seniors, we postulants made many remarks about the bathing suits. If one stood up in the water, you could see several humps of light blue and aqua trekking through the water! It was hysterical! We would laugh because of

Throwaway Nun

Rosemary Scirocco-Corsale
Kathleen A. Barreca

all the aborted efforts to swim. Sometimes our sides would hurt from all the laughing. Meanwhile, the mistress would be looking down at us from the very top next to the covered steps. Although we never told her what our opinions were of the bathing suits, it seems that Mother Pietra would come to find out for herself. When the senior nuns were swimming, we were not permitted near the manse. Very often the postulants' time to descend to the lake came immediately after that of the senior nuns. The nuns would leave the wet suits on the banister at each landing. The suits would still be wet when we got our chance in the water. Each person would stand on each landing in between the flight of steps and don the suit, wet or dry. They would call down to the next level to ask if they were finished dressing. When everyone on each of the four landings was ready, they would go to the beach, and then the second group would get dressed in the bathing suits. I was always in the last group. Although it was not pleasant to put on wet bathing suits, once in the water we were refreshed and relaxed. We were able to wash our hair, bathe, and frolic in the water! The suits were never washed; they were hung on the banisters to dry and to be worn by the next group of senior nuns or postulants. All of this wonderful recreation came to an end in September—we were never permitted to swim again. It seems that Rome learned of this activity and forbade its continuation. And so the fun in the water came to an end by the beginning of the school year in September, 1951. However, we would always laugh when we spoke of the infamous, waterproof bathing suits!

It was in the later part of spring, 1953, that I learned that I would be receiving the habit of the Order in June. I was ecstatic! However, my reactions had to be thwarted and very subdued because I feared that I would be again denied if I showed myself too joyful. I doubled my prayers

Throwaway Nun

Rosemary Scirocco-Corsale
Kathleen A. Barreca

and my daily efforts to be submissive and obedient. I was often overtaken with waves of panic and fear during this time. I thought that if I ever did anything to displease Mother Pietra, I would be sent home. So I tried to be very low keyed; I tried very hard to do everything so well that there would never be any occasion for the senior nuns to report me to her. Of all my years in the convent, this was the first truly "happy" time! I was not as severely depressed, and I was able to concentrate on daily matters. Shortly after I received the good news about my investiture, I learned that the graduating class of 1953 also would be receiving the habit of the Order. Now I fully understood why I was made to wait an entire year to receive mine! It was not that I was immature and not ready in 1952. The truth of the matter was that Mother Pietra did not consider me worthy enough of all the plans and preparations necessary for vestition for only me! This delay which was intended to degrade the importance of my person didn't matter now; I was glowing inside! I wrote a letter home to tell my family the good news. Their reply was that I could expect most of my family to attend, and as usual, they would come laden with foodstuffs for the convent.

That day, the 13th of July, 1953, was a very happy one for me. The chapel was decorated with church fineries and fresh flowers. The landing outside the rooms to the left of the manse had been rearranged. There was a temporary altar, kneelers covered with white satin fabric, and fresh flowers and ferns. The aisle leading to the kneelers was arrayed with a long, running, red carpet. White drapes were hung from the doorjambs and were tied back with sprigs of flowers and ferns. It all seemed to me like a piece of heaven had been dropped from the sky and came to rest on this very spot in Derby!

Throwaway Nun   **Rosemary Scirocco-Corsale**
                                                                                 Kathleen A. Barreca

Besides the members of my family, the relatives of the other postulants receiving the habit also arrived that day. There were many friends and benefactors of the Order. They all gathered on the lawn to the left of the manse. There were more than 200 people present. We five receiving our habits were escorted to the second floor of the manse. There we were helped into long, white dresses and white bridal veils. Instead of a bouquet of flowers, we were given a stack of clothing, our habit, and a black belt coiled on top. These we carried as we descended the stairs and walked slowly outside toward the chapel. During the ceremony, Mother Pietra stood behind each of us and handed us back each part of the habit after it had been blessed. When the blessed habit had been given to each postulant, we arose and filed back into the manse. We marched to the second floor. With the help of a senior nun, we donned the habit. We had black veils instead of white ones which is usual among all other Orders. When we emerged from the various rooms and saw each other dressed as a nun, we were all agog and very verbal about our "ohs" and "ahs!" In fact, a nun came up to tell us all to keep down the voices because we could be heard outside. We then walked down the steps and slowly wound our way back to the temporary chapel. As we filed past our families and relatives, we could hear the gentle weeping and subdued sobs. We heard the exclamations and the sighs. We knelt for the final part of the ceremony and the presentation of the newly vested nuns. Each maintained our given Christian name; henceforth, I would be called Sr. Rosemary. My family beamed with pride and joy. When we had our meal with our families, one of my brothers jokingly stated that I would always be "Babe," my family nickname. My father took by brother to task. He insisted that I be called with the title of respect, "Sister." The day was wonderful, beautiful, and

Throwaway Nun

Rosemary Scirocco-Corsale
Kathleen A. Barreca

happy. It was one of the extremely rare days that I was not degraded or berated. Because I had learned how to be totally subdued and obedient, my exuberance was internal and my joy was manifested by my smile on the external side. Toward evening, the festivities were over and the families, relatives, guests, and benefactors began to leave. It was the end of a very full day. That night, we would sleep in the coach house instead of in the gatehouse. In accordance with the Constitution of the Daughters of the Holy Word, we were referred to as "little sisters;" that is, the nuns waiting for the novitiate. In Italian, the word is suorina; however, to the lay person there appeared no difference between the full-fledged nun and us. We would not wear white veils even during novitiate because of the nature of the work we nuns did. Since they worked with printing materials, inks, oils, etc., white was not a practical color to wear.

The next morning, it was just wonderful to put on the habit! We had learned to kiss each piece before donning it. When we emerged from our rooms, even though we were to have grand silence, we smiled at one another. In chapel, we were instructed to sit in the pew behind the postulants. We were assigned our tasks after breakfast; mine was to sweep the floor in the large corridor from the foyer to the chapel. Sr. Angela passed by during the sweeping. She stated that the habit always made postulants look differently, but that I was the one that looked the most changed. She just looked at me and smiled, shaking her head from side to side. I said, "thank you." Immediately, the unkind names and constant degrading ceased. This caused me much concern internally, though I dared not discuss my worries with anyone. After investiture, I was never called even one of those unkind names again. I am sure that the end of the name calling was in deference to my wearing the habit! After my investiture, I was not verbally berated, until the end of my convent days. Again, this was not because my superiors had finally accepted my personhood, but rather for the respect of the habit. There is no doubt that Mother Pietra gave those nuns who were doing these unchristian like things orders to stop so as not to scandalize the postulants and aspirants. Although very leery, I was pleased at this turn of events. But, this was of short duration.

Soon after my vestition, we had retreats and with them were meditations, and the dreaded "passing." The following are excerpts of notes from that time:

July 15, 1952 - Retreat Meditation. Sunday, July 13, an unforgettable day in my life: I received the religious habit of the Daughters of St. Paul. It was the happiest day of my life. I want this retreat to be a turning point in my life! The Retreat Master: "These five new sisters are worthy of praise and honor. Many people think because you are sisters you are dead, but I say you are alive. You are just beginning to live! Your whole life is ahead of you. People may say you are wasting your time buried in a convent. They might say that it would be better if you would go home. Well, don't listen because it is the devil. In the convent you are happy. You are not wasting any time, but you are using all the time you have for the service of God. In the convent, live simply. Be obedient to the superiors and equals. Love one another. All during the month we fight with the devil. Once a month we retreat; that is, we go back to God who washes our wounds and give us more strength for another battle. During the retreat there should be only God on your mind. Only you and God exist in a retreat. If God is secondary, you are headed downhill, and you lose the battle. God must be the foremost thought regardless of all other circumstances or conditions. The salvation of our souls is the most important thing of life. Retreat is like taking inventory; we find out what we need, what is missing, what is damaged, and what needs to be replaced. It is an inventory of the whole month. 'Making the headlines' in heaven is all that matters in this life. Pat yourself on the back at your success, and then bend your head and say, mea culpa, which means—my fault." (*This is an example of the type of brainwashing that was to permeate all teachings and conferences, and eventually affect all the days of my life.*)

July 20, 1952 - Meditation. Is it I, Lord, who is obstructing your work in my soul and in others? In religious life we must give up our own desires, wishes, and wills to conform ourselves to community life. I realize that what I have done is at fault. I ask our Lord to amend my life, to give me the grace to be strong. We have many good qualities, but we have a few bad qualities which make the good qualities bad.

July 21, 1952 - Meditation. Mother Pietra says we must ask for a complete conversion from our predominant passions. I was told that mine was pride and distraction. If the Lord guards our senses, we need not worry. Let the Lord guard our senses so that we may use "our all energies" for Him. Mother Pietra said, "What energy? You look like old ladies. Let us have a little bit of energy! We must be exemplary, obedient missionaries. We must have a humble docility to all our superiors. When we obey, we are sure of doing God's will and of pleasing Him, thus winning over Satan. Within a month of my vestition, I was sent back to Staten Island where I had spent the first three sorrowful years of my convent life. The new "little sisters" had been informed that we would wait another year for novitiate. The others remained in Derby to continue working in the Apostolate. Someone else would learn how to operate the

Throwaway Nun

**Rosemary Scirocco-Corsale
Kathleen A. Barreca**

trimming machine. Someone else would have to do the lawn mowing, scraping the weeds of both sides of the road leading to the manse. Someone else would have to do all the manual work like packing the cases and boxes for shipping, lifting the heavy boxes, carrying anything from the station wagons, or doing what the superiors or senior nuns asked. I can remember when, sometime during 1952 before my receiving the habit on July 13, 1953, Mother Pietra came into the Apostolate with a photographer. Pictures were taken of the nuns working at the various machines. She passed the trimmer where I had been working, and proceeded to the other room which housed the linotype. Sr. Marie Terese asked why the trimming machine was not being photographed. Without turning back, Mother Pietra said, "We are only taking pictures of the important machines." Later, the trimmer would be photographed with another nun operating it (*I still have that picture*). The trimmer was an important machine; Mother Pietra just did not believe that I, the person who was operating it at that time, was important! It didn't matter how or what I felt. This was just another example of how poorly I was treated.

While I was in Staten Island, I came to learn about the situation back in Derby: the lawn was mowed over a period of several days, and always with the seat attached to the mower; the road was not cleared of weeds because the job was too difficult; when boxes had to be packed for shipment, many hands as possible were called upon to help because the work was too hard for just one or two people. When I received this information from one of the senior nuns passing through Staten Island on her way to Louisiana, I thought it was very strange. These jobs were all performed by me, alone! For a few days, I ruminated on this and began to feel a wave of anger wash over me. I was beginning to realize that I was

Throwaway Nun

not being treated as the others. I had been in the convent for five years. These thoughts permeated the things I did every day. At the end of these few days, I became overwhelmed with guilt. I had no right to have these thoughts; I had no right to think that any treatment of me was unkind, unchristian like, or religiously unbecoming. I prayed doubly hard for forgiveness for what I thought were sins and temptations from the devil, himself. I was thankful when these thoughts left me. Unwittingly, I was buying into the "mystique" of the authority of everyone around me!

Sr. Clara was the Superior in Staten Island when I was sent there. I was the only "young" sister there; all the others were senior nuns with many years of convent life. I was gaining some peace and tranquility as the weeks progressed, and I was not called unkind names and berated constantly. I was assigned many of the heavy tasks, but not the laundry. I had to keep the cellar cleaned, the shelves stocked with books and pamphlets; package all requests for printed materials to individuals, stores, and lay libraries; and unpack the many boxes sent there from Derby. Shortly after my arrival, shipments of books were mostly untrimmed. There was a very old, very slow trimming machine in the cellar at Staten Island. It was so old that it was the only piece of equipment not sent to Derby in 1950. During one of her visits, Mother Pietra ordered me to the cellar to learn how to operate this old trimmer (*if I learned how to use this machine, then Derby could ship all the paperback books and other items untrimmed to Staten Island*). And, that is exactly what was done! I would spend many evenings at the trimmer. When Mother Pietra was "teaching" me to operate this piece of antiquity, she stated that the blade was very sharp and fast, and that I had to be very careful. I was standing right next to her and I could see how slowly the blade descended, how difficult it

Throwaway Nun

Rosemary Scirocco-Corsale
Kathleen A. Barreca

was to trim even a small stack of books, and how the trimmed edges of the books had ridges which indicated that the blade was not sharp and had probably seen its better days. After she had said this, I jerked my head to the right to look at her. As usual, she avoided eye contact. When left alone to work at the trimmer, I silently wondered why she had so deliberately lied, and why she tried to scare me. Why had she continued to think I was stupid? If Mother Pietra still thought of me as mammalucca, that is, a retard, then why had she granted total approval for my investiture of the habit! A wave of panic swept over me—if she had perceived my doubts, read the incredulousness in the jerking of my head, she was sure to subject me to one of her now-famous berating and degrading before the entire community of nuns. I waited for the fallout, but it never came. I thanked God profusely in my prayers! So, the work in the cellar, cleaning the floors, sweeping, dusting, and other manual tasks became my lot. At the same time, a very different form of degrading began to take shape.

During the monthly retreats, Sr. Clara began telling me that the reason why I was the only little sister sent away from Derby was because I was such a bad example to my peers and to the postulants. I was instructed to talk less, be more obedient, and pray more. When she had told me about my being a menace to the other little sisters and the postulants several times, I became bold enough to ask in which specific areas I had transgressed. She dismissed my request with a shrug of her shoulders. After this, it seemed to me that she backed off. Instead, she became evermore a spiritual guide. She was motherly and solicitous in her spiritual remonstrations. With each retreat I actually looked forward to these conferences. It seemed that I blossomed spiritually. I felt that my prayer time was becoming more fruitful, that I was getting a solid hold on what it

Throwaway Nun Rosemary Scirocco-Corsale
Kathleen A. Barreca

meant to lose oneself to the will of God and to the mission of the Order. I became even more tolerant of the demands made on my time by the senior nuns (*I was always running this or the other errand for them*). I was, for the first time in my religious life, enjoying my days and nights in the convent. I had stopped crying myself to sleep shortly before I received the habit. Each day, six days a week, I went out into the greater New York area to sell books and pamphlets; beg for donations; seeking fabrics, materials, textiles, and other items to be sent to Italy or to be used in the United States. All the tasks assigned to me would be completed in the early mornings before breakfast and during evening hours after the dinner dishes were done. I did not dread coming back to the convent at the end of each day. If there were heavy things to carry back from the City, I would do more than my share.

Shortly after I arrived in New York, I was in need of a newer and better case in which to carry the books, pamphlets and various other religious literatures taken on the daily trips to sell in various boroughs of Greater Manhattan. The one I had was falling apart. I had to use black shoe polish to try to disguise the fact that the stitching was badly frayed, the four corners developed holes and the handles were badly torn apart. When I presented it to Sr. Clara, she agreed that I needed another one. That very day I was given a new one. It was made of leather. The case was larger than a briefcase and had three compartments inside. It closed with a zipper on the top, but I never used it. The case was referred to as a "propaganda bag." Sr. Clara was very careful when she opened the plastic to remove the new propaganda bag. Since the leather is stiff and firm at first, she used her fists and hands to get it to open fully. The next day when I went to get the bag to go into town with a senior nun, she followed

Throwaway Nun

Rosemary Scirocco-Corsale
Kathleen A. Barreca

me into the cellar. She took the bag from my hand and placed it on the table. Then she began unjustified accusations that I did not fill the bag because I had deliberately tried to keep it "new" and in good shape. She then got several books, pamphlets, etc., and tried to stuff them into the bag. But none would fit. She succeeded in placing a single pamphlet into it, expressing her satisfaction with her efforts. I simply stood by and said nothing. When she had finished, she said I could go upstairs and go out with the senior nun.

About three months later, most all the nuns were in the cellar preparing their bags for the next day. One of the senior nuns jokingly put her bag on an ancient scale which sat on a wooden table in the small corridor. As others put their bags on the scale, there was much laughing and joking. The weights were from 9 to 17 pounds. As usual I was on the fringe of the group and did not participate in the many comments. Suddenly, Sr. Clara turned to me and ordered me to bring my bag to the scale. Needless to say I was somewhat apprehensive because I was being set up for a public humiliation. When the recently acquired bag was put on the scale it weighed 34 pounds! There was an instant hush among the nuns. No one said a word. Sr. Clara quickly took the bag off the scale and handed it to me. Everyone then disbanded from around the scale. I carried this bag every day of the week, except Sundays. In addition, I was expected to carry most of the items donated throughout the day, like food items, scraps of cloth, etc. By the end of the day most of the contents of the bag had been sold for financial donations, therefore I was able to place many items right into the bag. Once I went to the special area of town which several pairs of nuns visited every Saturday. Most people were Irish and held nuns in great reverence. They were, also, very generous. I had

Throwaway Nun

**Rosemary Scirocco-Corsale
Kathleen A. Barreca**

been paired with a young senior nun who had experienced medical problems in the past. I deliberately made every effort to carry everything the good people donated to us that day. It wasn't easy. My cloth bag which covered the open propaganda bag was stuffed and I was forced to carry it on my arm without any reprieve. I could see that Sr. Mary was grimacing when she lifted her bag. We went into a store and she placed her bag on the floor against a post. I lifted her bag because I was anxious to help alleviate her burden. When I did so the bag was so light, I nearly jerked it off the floor. On the way out Sr. Mary began to complain that her bag was too heavy and she did not know if she would have the strength to finish the day. I looked at her and said words I never thought I would ever say. I said, "Would you like to carry my bag?" Our eyes locked. She was as taken aback by the comment as I was in making it. However, she never responded. Rather, we finished the day and returned to the convent at dusk with the others. I was sure that she was going to tell Sr. Clara and that I had undeliberately set myself up for another upbraiding and public humiliation. However, not one word was said. Sr. Mary had not said anything to anyone.

I was very pleasantly surprised when Sr. Clara told me that I would be going to Providence, Rhode Island with Sr. Adele. It seemed that a predominantly Italian parish wanted to have the church census taken. At the same time, we could sell our books to the parishioners. We were to leave soon after the monthly retreat in October. We had packed several boxes of books, pamphlets, and religious items such as medals and rosary beads. On a Sunday, we were taken to LaGuardia Airport in New York City, and arrived in Providence shortly thereafter. We took a taxi to the parish house and announced our arrival. Sr. Adele had been informed that

Throwaway Nun

**Rosemary Scirocco-Corsale
Kathleen A. Barreca**

the parish priest would have already made arrangements for us to stay in a private home. The home was a second story apartment of a very devout, elderly widow who was 78 years of age. She dyed her hair with henna and wore it in a bun. She kept a very tidy house, and we were shown to the first bedroom. There was a double bed, and we would have to sleep together. I had learned years ago to lie on my back with my hands crossed over my chest clutching a pair of rosary beads. I never moved; I was always so tired that I fell asleep soon after my head hit the pillow. This lady's apartment was in a home almost directly behind the church rectory. So, it took me about three or four trips to bring all the boxes upstairs and into our bedroom. Sr. Adele socialized with the lady while I put the packages in place. We attended Mass each morning in the church, and returned to the apartment where this nice lady had coffee and toast prepared for us. Then, we would go out and knock on every door. This went on as we canvassed street after street. There was another Roman Catholic Church within two blocks of the Italian parish. As we talked to people and received the census information from them, we also received some lessons in the history, bigotry, and violence of their town. It seems that the Irish residents of Providence did not like the fact that their parish was being inundated by Italian immigrants. So, they had their own church built less than two blocks away. When the influx of Italian immigrants was at its peak, so the story goes, the Irish men would kill Italian men or boys who were walking alone, especially at night. It seems that this bigotry and violence had some merit in truth because we met the relatives of a few of those who were slain. In taking the census, we crossed the thresholds of second and third generation Italians who belonged to the "Irish Church and some who had married individuals of Irish descent and

Throwaway Nun

**Rosemary Scirocco-Corsale
Kathleen A. Barreca**

other nationalities who belonged there, too. It seemed that there was some sort of prestige associated with belonging to the "other" church. There was great rivalry between the members of these two churches. The base of this conflict had to do with the "old country" values, customs, traditions, and cooking. Those Italians most anxious to acculturate and abandon their parents' and grandparents' customs to became "Americanized." Belonging to the Irish Church was announcing the break with tradition and becoming Americanized. Whenever we encountered families belonging to the Irish Church, we would not take the census and never tried to talk them into going to the original church. The people were very kind and accommodating, regardless of which church they attended.

Even though the season was fall in Rhode Island, these were two days of very oppressive, stifling heat! It was difficult to breathe, and it took extra strength to walk. Many homes had window air conditioners, and when we exited these homes, it seemed that the air was more putrid and oppressive than before. Everyone offered us something to drink. My throat always felt dry, and with Sr. Adele's permission, I had several drinks on the second day. It was so hot and unbearable that Sr. Adele stopped early and we went to the apartment where we were staying. The hostess had made supper for us, and we retired early. As soon as I got into bed, I jumped up and ran to the bathroom. I almost made it, but I soiled the throw rugs. I vomited my supper, all that I had to drink that day, and I thought, the lining of my stomach, too! My head reeled and my knees were weak. I sat on the edge of the bathtub for a while. I gathered up the two throw rugs and washed them in the bathtub. When they had been rinsed, I hung them on the line which was strung from outside the bathroom window to the house behind this one (*the lines reminded me of*

Throwaway Nun

Rosemary Scirocco-Corsale
Kathleen A. Barreca

those on the tenement buildings in New York City). I went to our bedroom where Sr. Adele was already in bed. I tried to be very still so as not to disturb her. Neither that night nor the next day did she ask me how I felt or if I needed any medical attention.

After about one week, Sr. Adele told me to do the laundry in the bathtub (*the lady did not own a washer or dryer*). She then told me to hang the clothes on the line to dry. I was humiliated and very embarrassed. The rectory and other houses were located at the rear of this house. If anyone looked out their windows, they would see the underclothing of the nuns, which were very different from the lingerie used by the laity. I was ordered to hang the clothing out and to retrieve them when they were dry.

Within that same week, we were taking the census on streets which were a distance from the apartment where we were staying. Therefore, the parish priest made arrangements for us to stay at a convent of teaching nuns. They were from an Italian-founded order and consisted of a Mother Superior and two other nuns. We stayed at the convent for four days, and we had our breakfast and dinner with them. On the third day, I was stunned when Sr. Adele began degrading me to these nuns. She complained that I was too talkative, disobedient, immature, and a bad example to everyone. The nuns were obviously taken aback by this outpouring. I had been amid them for three days and they knew very well that I was not the person that Sr. Adele was describing. While she was lamenting about my faults and sins, I could feel the piercing looks from these nuns. I looked up once and saw all of them looking at me; I just lowered my head. When Sr. Adele had finished her diatribe, Mother Superior told her that everyone had faults; she immediately changed the subject. I was inwardly distraught with this turn of events. What had made

Throwaway Nun

Rosemary Scirocco-Corsale
Kathleen A. Barreca

her say these untrue and vicious things—and to a group of proverbial strangers! They had never experienced nor observed the kind of behavior from me that Sr. Adele was describing. Again, my stomach tightened, and I swallowed the humiliation, the unjust accusations, and embarrassment. A while later, I was to learn that Sr. Adele could barely read and write! The teaching nuns all knew that I had been doing all the writing of the census, organizing the data cards, and submitting the completed ones to the parish priest. This eruption might have been her effort to show who was in charge, who maintained the upper hand. I was just her sidekick; I was also her victim!

We had completed the census around the area of the convent of the teaching nuns, and again, the parish priest had arranged for us to stay with one of his parishioners. She was divorced, never remarried, and had no children. She worked in a local factory. Her apartment was on the second floor above a store. I can still remember that it was on Balboa Avenue. Until this point in my life, I had read and heard about very saintly lay persons, but this lady was my first encounter with lay sanctity. Her apartment had one double bed and one chest of drawers. In the kitchen there was a small table with two chairs and a refrigerator. There were sundry dishes, pots and pans, silverware, and other similar items. However, one got the impressions that she rarely used these things. In fact, that was the case! There was no other furniture in the apartment, and she slept on the living room floor. The living room was empty except for in the right corner where there were at least 30 statues of Jesus, the Blessed Mother, and various saints. She explained that she had collected all of these over a number of years from the families of deceased relatives, people who were modernizing their homes and no longer wanted the

Throwaway Nun

Rosemary Scirocco-Corsale
Kathleen A. Barreca

statues, and even from a couple of local Roman Catholic churches which were replacing their icons with new or larger ones. From persons in the immediate area and then from her own lips, we learned that she lived this way because she wanted to sacrifice for the good of others. She would give her salary away to various charities and to those in need. She fasted so arduously that she passed out on her job. She was known to be kind and gentle with everyone. No one could recall ever hearing her utter an unkind or impatient word. So goes sainthood! Though her apartment was devoid of anything superfluous, there was an aura of the sublime in that place! I felt it more here than in the convent. She was so honored to have us stay at her home. She stocked the refrigerator so that we could cook our meals in her kitchen; we did just that for the entire week we stayed there. Although it was autumn, there were some very hot and humid days. One evening, Sr. Adele and I sat down to our evening meal that we prepared. We had opened a bottle of a famous brand of cola and poured half into each glass. The cola was warm, but Sr. Adele made no effort to get some ice cubes from the refrigerator, and I dared not to. I was very thirsty, so after our prayer, I took a large gulp of the cola. I leaped from the chair and went to the sink and spit out the contents of my mouth. In disgust and horror I watched as a mouthful of someone's sputum slithered slowly down the drain! The sputum had been in the cola bottle! I was sick to my stomach; I held on to the sink with both hands. When I was sure I would not get sick again, I threw the leftover cola in my glass down the drain. Sr. Adele never said a word and never asked if anything was wrong. From that day until I am laid to my eternal rest, I have not nor will I ever drink any brand of cola; I have come to drink a lot of water!

Throwaway Nun

Rosemary Scirocco-Corsale
Kathleen A. Barreca

We returned to the apartment of the elderly lady for the last couple of days of that month. One evening after a hard-working day, our host had prepared a dessert for us. She had put canned peach halves on slices of pound cake. There were three servings on a plate. Sr. Adele and I had carefully placed a serving on our plate. We noticed that the third serving had a strand of her long, dyed hair in between the peach and the pound cake! When we had finished our dessert, the kind lady insisted that we share the remaining one. We graciously declined, but the hostess would not accept our refusals. With a smirk on her face, Sr. Adele looked squarely into my eyes and ordered me to eat it! I had to obey. I had trained myself never to react, never to disregard an order. I placed the offending dessert on my plate and I pulled the strand of hair out from under the peach. I held it up to shoulder height and let it fall to the floor. Then I ate the dessert. I wondered why Sr. Adele had been so cruel, and why she would get any kind of satisfaction from seeing me in that predicament. Needless to say, I have never eaten peaches and pound cake combination since.

Sr. Adele then informed me that we were leaving Providence and returning to Staten Island for our monthly retreat. We arrived on the last day of the month; the next day was Sunday, November 1, 1953. After dinner, I was called aside and told that my oldest sister, Carmel, had died suddenly that morning. She was 26 years old and had been married less than two years. The next morning, I left by train for Youngstown. I arrived there either late in the afternoon or early evening. The next day, I was accompanied to the funeral home by Sr. Eduarde. My mother, who had discovered my sister's body, was still in a state of shock. The other members of my family were mourning, to say the least. This was the first

Throwaway Nun

**Rosemary Scirocco-Corsale
Kathleen A. Barreca**

time I had met Carmel's husband, Frank. His eyes were red and swollen; we just embraced. When I knelt before the coffin, the tears started rolling down my cheeks. This, after all, was my favorite sister. She had really favored me. When I regained my composure, Sr. Eduarde nudged me and told me to say the rosary aloud. I did not think I would be able to do so because of the lump in my throat and of fighting back the tears. Nevertheless, I obeyed. To this day, I cannot explain how I was able to complete saying the rosary! Just a month prior to her death, she had written me such a wonderful letter; it read:

"Dear Sister Rosemary,

How are things? I don't have a thing to do right now, so I thought I'd write to you. I am feeling so much better and happier. I know now you have been praying for me, and your prayers and mine were answered. Frank and I are so busy getting our house ready. My sister-in-law, Marie, is making my drapes. Sophie has bought me a table lamp. It's so big and so beautiful—I can't wait to use it. Ang [our sister, Angie] made me a crochet doily set, and Mom and Pa bought us our kitchen set. Oh, Sister, do I really deserve all this? Maybe it is Mt. Carmel's way of telling me not to worry anymore. Everyone is so good. We might be in our house for sure, anyway, in January. Ang doesn't know what she is going to do without me at home. And neither does Mom. Sister, they were really crying last week because I'm moving. And I got mad because, after all, I'm only going like say from Girard to Youngstown. Ang says she comes down the house to see Mom and Pa, but we both spend the evening together. We talk about everything. And Mom said it is going to be so hard for her to do the work I do. I wash part of her clothes with mine, I make her sleep in the afternoon,

Throwaway Nun

Rosemary Scirocco-Corsale
Kathleen A. Barreca

and I see that everything is taken care of. I mean if something is cooking on the stove, I take care of it for her. I do her ironing. I clean the house. So, I guess she will miss me.

We made wine and is it good. Johnny [our brother] bought the grapes. You would split your sides laughing. Your Godmother, Yolanda, loaned us the grape crusher machine, and she and Johnny took turns turning the handle. And every time Johnny took over, he would make us laugh. He'd say to Mom or to Yolanda, 'Don't put in too many grapes, after all, I'm not Superman,' or else, 'Put in more grapes, I don't want to be here all day,' and then, 'Ain't we done yet, my muscle fell off in one arm already.' Can you picture Johnny standing on one foot, smoking and always saying, 'Are we done,' 'Are we done?' Yes, that's him. He was a card. Now that the wine is made, he keeps asking, 'When can we drink it?' and 'You mean to tell me it isn't ready to drink yet?' He's a nut head.

Oh, I better stop right here. We're all fine. Write to me soon. I like to hear from you, and so does the family.
Love always,
Carmel and Frank,
God bless you."

She and her husband had just completed building their dream house. They were to have moved into it on December 1, but she did not live until then. The next day, I attended the funeral. After the burial rite at the cemetery, I bent to kiss her coffin and took a red rose from the blanket bouquet. I pressed it between the pages of one of my prayer books when I returned to Staten Island. All of my religious training and prayer life had come into focus for me. My heart was crushed, but I considered the sad faces and the red, swollen eyes of my parents and the rest of my family. More than me, they would need the help of the Heavenly Choirs, of the Lord who is consolation, Himself; and His Blessed Mother. Therefore, I had to remain as calm and collected as possible....for their sakes. I could mourn internally (*where I learned to process all the things in my life*). When we had returned to my parents' home after the funeral, my sister's husband, Frank, presented me with her wallet, but it would have been a human link to my dead sister. There was hurt in Frank's eyes. I knew that if I had taken the wallet, it would have been taken from me as soon as I arrived at Staten Island. I would never be permitted to keep it. After saying "good-bye" to my family, I returned to the convent in Youngstown, and the following day went back to New York. None of the nuns, not even Sr. Clara, rendered condolences! No one said they would pray for her soul. The next day, I was out selling books again. I prayed every day for my family to be given the strength to endure this great loss, and I prayed that my dear sister be brought into the Glory of Paradise.

I continued to keep notes especially the advices and admonishing of my superiors. Just before my sister's death, I wrote the following:

August, 1953 - Meditations. I shall accept all corrections with humility or at least I will not show my feelings exteriorly. If I do, I shall say that I am sorry.

September 6, 1953 - St. Paul said, "The will of God is your sanctification." The soul is perfected by performing God's will.

This month I did not accept all the corrections. I showed my feelings because I esteem myself too much and feel I don't deserve them. I feel as though I am not trusted with anything. Humility is the first step toward

Throwaway Nun

Rosemary Scirocco-Corsale
Kathleen A. Barreca

self-surrender. This month I shall convince myself that I deserve all the corrections I receive.

October 4, 1953 - By faithful recitation of the rosary and meditation, one can be led to a great degree of perfection. Fraternal charity is one of the most important factors of religious life to maintain the true spirits and to sanctify oneself.

I kept many notes of retreats, meditations, conferences and especially "passing's." I took these very seriously, especially those accusations, humiliations and degrading by my superiors. I re-read and reviewed them often.

Sometime in early spring of 1954, I was sent to New Bedford, Massachusetts, with Sr. Peter to take the census in a Portuguese parish. Sr. Peter was from Brazil, South America, and could communicate with the Portuguese-speaking people of this community. Arrangements had been made for us to stay in the convent of the nuns who taught in the parochial school belonging to the parish. This community had never had any member of the clergy or religious visit them or call at their homes. The first reaction of most people was one of amazement and shock. Within a week, the word had spread throughout the parish that we were going from home to home. Most importantly, they had begun telling each other that we accepted invitations to lunch and/or dinner. I cannot tell how many invitations we had to decline and how disappointed the persons were who invited us. Lunches and dinners were elaborate and sumptuous. The women prepared delicious Portuguese desserts which were fit for royalty. It seemed that it became a "badge of prestige" for them to have us in their homes for a meal. More than once, the family would drive us to the home of a relative outside the parish, and most family members would be

Throwaway Nun

Rosemary Scirocco-Corsale
Kathleen A. Barreca

present, just like on a major holiday. Very little English was spoken during these occasions. One of the things I learned about these very warm and gentile people was that they had a very great devotion to the Holy Spirit. I cannot recall one home that did not have a silver dove in a glass dome *(the silver dove is the representation of the Holy Spirit)*. Some doves were larger than others; whatever the case, they were prominently displayed on the dining buffet or on a table in the living room. In our travels throughout the parish, we met people who were too ill to attend church. Until our visit, they had not requested visitations from the parish priest or to receive the Sacraments. We would, therefore, give the names and addresses to the pastor as soon as possible. Everyone thought that this was a miracle in the community!

Sr. Peter was a very gentile, sensitive nun. She was actually fun to be with. She never kept silences, and enjoyed telling stories. She was a great raconteur, and the way she recounted tales of her experiences in Brazil made everyone laugh. She was one of the senior nuns who never caused me any grief, never tried to ingratiate herself to Mother Pietra, and made her own decisions. When she was suddenly sent back to Brazil in 1957, I was very surprised and saddened. Much later, I was to learn that she was apprehended taking some of the money from each senior nun's pouches in the counting room. It seems that she dealt with Mother Pietra and those who were her pets by proffering the largest monetary take for each day she went out selling books! I was in New York and watched as she was hustled into the station wagon and whisked off to the airport. However, she was never publicly humiliated or berated for her actions. Neither was she ever dismissed from the convent. She was, simply, "sent elsewhere."

Throwaway Nun

Rosemary Scirocco-Corsale
Kathleen A. Barreca

Although Sr. Clara would take me to task for my faults and shortcomings during the monthly conferences, she never made me the laughing stock of the community. She did, however, think of me as having very limited intelligence. While this was the idea about my person perpetuated by Mother Pietra and her favorite nuns (*most supportively, Sr. Constance*), I unwittingly allowed Sr. Clara to actually experience how lowly I thought of myself. While I was still a postulant in Derby, New York, between 1951 and 1952, I was ordered to accompany her to Buffalo. She informed me that we were going to see the Bishop at the Chancery Office, and that I was to wear my "Sunday" clothes. In between running errands in the city, she made me eat my lunch though she never touched hers; she was driving. During these many years of my being brainwashed, one of the things pounded into my head was to always smile, be reserved, and talk very little. The key word here is "always." I had already trained myself to blind obedience and submission. The smiling, as I was told, was to let other clergy know that we were very happy in the convent of the Daughters of the Holy Word. We arrived at the Chancery Office right after lunch and we were escorted into the Bishop's office. Immediately, I put on a big smile and kept the smile on my face while Sr. Clara and he talked. I remember the strange look on his face every time he looked at me. The visit was mercifully brief; my jaws were hurting from all of the smiling. When we were in the station wagon, Sr. Clara handed me her lunch and ordered me to eat it. In disbelief, I took the lunch from her hands. I had just eaten my own huge lunch less than two hours ago. Why would she order me to eat again? She and I both knew that I would have to eat supper within hours and that I would not be given permission to excuse myself from the dinner table. I thought this command, on her part, was cruel. By

Throwaway Nun

Rosemary Scirocco-Corsale
Kathleen A. Barreca

now, I had learned to say nothing and to assess everything internally. It occurred to me that the pasted smile on my face while visiting with the Bishop looked ridiculous; it made me look retarded. The order that Sr. Clara gave me to eat her huge lunch was her way of nonverbally agreeing with the conclusion the Bishop had reached. Never again would I ever accompany anyone to the Chancery Office; never would I ever be sent to be with or communicate with any religious, parish priest, or missionary. There was no way I could undo the damage of that day. I learned, however, that I did not need to keep the smile on my face continuously. How blindly obedient I had become! Hence, when Sr. Clara, as the Mother Superior of Staten Island, became my superior, she had total jurisdiction over me. I thought of her as kinder as and gentler than Mother Pietra, Sr. Constance, and several other nuns whom I knew to be spies. My respect for Sr. Clara grew also out of the fact that she did not deliberately and maliciously degrade me before the whole community. When I had been given the habit of the Order, I began to keep a very personal diary. Into this little book I would write my innermost thoughts and feelings. Between these private pages I could describe my emotions and reactions to the humiliations, what my heart was holding spiritually, and where I wanted my journey to the Lord to go. I also wrote about senior nuns without naming them. This was not true of Sr. Constance; I was clear in writing her name. I often hid this small book being fearful that someone would find it and give it to Mother Pietra, or take it from the repository where we kept our prayer books. I had been told that I would soon be going back to Derby to begin my novitiate, which was to start at the end of June, 1954. I thought that maybe, just maybe, I could trust Sr. Clara, and I gave her my diary to read. I had discussed with her the idea that we might talk about

Throwaway Nun

Rosemary Scirocco-Corsale
Kathleen A. Barreca

the contents before I returned to Derby. Several days later, Sr. Clara stopped me at the foot of the stairs. We were alone. She took my small book out of her pocket and handed it to me. With a scowl on her forehead and firmness in her voice I had not heard before, she proceeded to tell me that I was full of self-pity, ungenerous, not dedicated to the Order, and not respectful of the senior nuns. She further told me that Sr. Constance was a saint, and that my own sinfulness made me see her in the negative way I had written about her. While I took the book from her hand, she ordered me to go into the steam room, open the door to the furnace, and burn every page of the book. I knew that furnace room very well; in late spring and winter it was one of my many jobs to stoke the furnace each morning and to fill the bin which fed small pieces of coal into it. I removed the ashes and brought them to the end of the road for trash pickup every week. The smell, the misty view of the room, the dimness of the 25-watt bulb in the unshaded, hanging light; the grayness of the floor caused by the ashes are so vivid, my senses betray me because I think it was just yesterday. I opened the furnace door and I stood there motionless for some time. Then, one by one, I tore out the pages and watched each one be consumed by the fire. With each page a small part of my heart was being burned. As each page burned, I could feel the tears welling in my eyes, and my throat burned. I had trusted, I had let down my guard, I had stopped being paranoid for a very short time. As the flames enveloped these precious pages, I felt betrayed to the very marrow of my bones. I verbally chastised myself for opening up, for letting someone in my inner world. This small book was the only thing I had that contained the internal self, my thoughts, my feelings, my emotions, my reactions, my covert world, my one avenue of sanity amid the mental, spiritual, and physical abuse. I lay between the

Throwaway Nun

Rosemary Scirocco-Corsale
Kathleen A. Barreca

pages of that book; I could walk, sleep, and think within it without fear of reprisal. And now, this book that was so precious to me was considered a heap of bunk! It was considered a matter of trash and self-pity, not worthy enough even to talk about, even to discuss. And, I had been ordered to burn it—not even to throw it in the trash! My persona had been assaulted, my inner self reduced to nothingness, my thoughts dismissed as having no merit. If I had thrown myself into the fire that day, the pain and agony of burning would not reach an iota of the anguish I was undergoing in my soul. When I threw the last back page into the flames, I resolved never again to trust anyone, to remain paranoid, never to share anything about my inner self with anyone, and never to commit a word in writing again. I kept these resolutions until a few months before my dismissal from the convent. No one ever saw these pages; I still have them. I would never again trust Sr. Clara; she had confirmed that I was not worth anything!

The following notes not only show self-debasement but also the continuation of verbal and emotional abuse.

September, 1953 - Resolutions. I shall accept all corrections with humility or at least I will not show my feelings exteriorly. If I do I shall say I'm sorry. The will of God is your sanctification. The soul is perfected by performing God's will. This month I did not accept all the corrections well. I showed my feelings because I see myself too much and I feel I don't deserve them. I feel as though I'm not trusted with anything. Resolution. Humility is the first step toward self-surrender. This month I shall convince myself that I deserve all the corrections I receive.

November 1, 1953. I wouldn't say I made a step forward as far as interior feelings are concerned, but this month the falls were less because I tried with all my heart to fight against my feelings and I put a strong effort behind the examination of conscience. I also tried to pray well, to meditate well. Whenever I don't receive a correction well, or don't fight my feelings, I shall consign myself to my superior.

December, 1953. This month I didn't show my feelings externally, but I had to fight internally because I thought I was right, that I knew more. I go forward sometimes and backwards at other times, just like Sr. Clara said. April, 1954. I shall receive all corrections with joy and serenity. I have tried this month to put into practice the advices given to me. At least this month I kept my resolution because I really do want to progress and become a saint. During this month of May, I shall be extra vigilant over myself, and I shall seek to imitate Blessed Mother's humility of heart by never reasoning or fantasticating on anything I am told, neither on corrections.

In June, 1954, I was sent to Derby to begin my novitiate. There I learned that Sr. Constance was to be our Mistress of Novices. I shuddered inside. During the seven day retreat which preceded the novitiate, I prayed mightily. I begged that the good Lord would change my heart toward her. He must have heard my supplications; I did not seem to possess the same dread. I was elated when I passed the "Canonical Visit" necessary to enter the novitiate year.

I was jubilant to be entering the novitiate. Simply to have been given the permission to begin this year was so gratifying and so satisfying that I resolved to put all the agonies and torments of the past behind me. I made up my mind that this would be the real beginning of my religious life. I reasoned that Mother Pietra had, after all, found some redeeming graces in me to allow me to enter this momentous year. If the name-calling had ceased with the donning of my habit, and if the two years

Throwaway Nun

**Rosemary Scirocco-Corsale
Kathleen A. Barreca**

spent in Staten Island had been reasonably good years, then the mental and psychological abuse would also cease once I made the Profession of Vows.

I would then be a full-fledged nun; I would be permitted into the places forbidden as a postulant and little sister. As a full-fledged nun, Mother Pietra and her spies would have very little to rebuke in me.

May, 1954. In preparation for the novitiate, I shall obey my superiors by subjecting my thoughts and opinions to theirs.

June 20, 1954. - The Retreat in Preparation for the Novitiate. I find during this past year four outstanding impediments which have caused me to make less progress than I did. 1) I consider myself good enough in a general way. 2) I was so distracted that I did not remember my resolutions half the times. 3) My pride, great pride, which is the cause of all my falls, is my predominant passion. 4) I did not even make an extra effort. I used so little of the willpower I have. I did not make as many gestures now as last month except when I laugh. As Sr. Constance said, I am still very distracted, and I know it only too well. But, during this month, I'll work on recollection as never before, especially during the apostolate time, 1) by observing silence; 2) by never looking around; 3) by doing my duty well, accompanied by many prayers. And so, with these positive emotions, hopeful expectations, and feelings, I began the year of the novitiate. There were six others; they would forever thereafter be known as my "co-novices." Pope Pius XII had declared 1954 as a special Holy Year; it would be known as the Marian Year. Pilgrims to Rome would be accorded the same special favors and blessings as those received during the Holy Year, and St. Peter's Door would again be opened. We seven had been told that we were a special group making our novitiate during a special year.

Throwaway Nun

Rosemary Scirocco-Corsale
Kathleen A. Barreca

We would be only the second group making our novitiate during a special year. We would be only the second group of novices to make the novitiate in the United States. Our superiors informed us over and over again that novices brought special blessings to the "House" (*meaning the convent*) during the year, and they expected more blessings with our group since it was the Marian Year.

My co-novices were not strangers to me. I had spent some time with them as postulants. In 1952, I had received the habit with four of them. Even though we had been apart, we developed a common bond usual among those who share similar experiences. I was very happy! I was a novice! Finally, after seven years, I was on the last leg of my journey to becoming a nun!

Just months before, when Sr. Clara had ordered me to destroy my diary, I had been made to feel that my feelings, thoughts, and opinions about Sr. Constance were wrong and that they had been inspired by the devil himself. Therefore, I was instructed to pray so that all these unkind feelings and thoughts would leave me and that I would see the holiness and sanctity of Sr. Constance. During those first couple of weeks in the novitiate, she was, in fact, very kind toward me. I prayed mightily that the devil would remove the "evil" thoughts and feelings from me. While I was mercifully spared from these inner conflicts in these early weeks, I remained tacit about my true inner self. I had just been through a most torturous, soul-wrenching experience in Staten Island when I let my guard down, tried to be trusting, and made an effort to seek the spiritual guidance of my superior. The entire experience of sharing the diary, being made to destroy it, and then the accusations and berating still burned in my heart. It did not take long for my suspicions to become a reality. After the

Throwaway Nun

**Rosemary Scirocco-Corsale
Kathleen A. Barreca**

first retreat and monthly conference, it seemed that the verbal chastisements, humiliations, and degrading picked up in Derby where they had left off when I had received the habit of the Order. I was not called the usual unkind names, but throughout the novitiate year I would be called "slow," unon-generous," and "lazy." I would be accused of being a bad example to my co-novices, postulants, and young aspirants, even though we never spoke with, associated with, or recreated with them. We would see them in the apostolate for a few hours during the week. However, the rules and regulations governing our behavior during our novice ship precluded any communication with them. I was accused of talking too much, laughing too loudly, always being distracted, and not having the true spirit of the Order. I never seemed to have any difficulties with my co-novices. They never avoided me; conversely, they talked with me, sought my input together with others, and did not perceive me as a bad example to them. Very early in the novitiate, I understood that, again, I would be a scapegoat and a whipping post; I would be abused emotionally and mentally. Inwardly, I again panicked and waves of depression would be my lot. I asked myself over and over again if I would have the intestinal fortitude to endure this assault on my total person. I prayed intensely for this fortitude and courage. I loved the religious life; I really loved the evangelization mission of the Order. I enjoyed working at making and binding books, even though the workload given me was harder than that given others. I would never ask to go home! I would never ask to leave; in spite of the torture and torment, I wanted to become a nun!

In preparation for the novitiate, I wrote the following during the retreat in June: Novitiate 1954. When you enter the convent, you leave the world; when you enter the novitiate, you leave the ego! The novitiate is

Throwaway Nun

Rosemary Scirocco-Corsale
Kathleen A. Barreca

the time in which the aspiring studies the congregation to see if she is called; and likewise, the congregation studies the aspirant to see if she has the qualities to live in the religious state. The novice must 1) study the religious state well; 2) study the catechism; 3) study esthetics so that she may know Jesus' truth. During the novitiate, we must practice the vows and the religious virtues, that is, poverty, chastity, and community life. Don't ever ask for exceptions or for personal affairs that take you away from the group, except for the necessity of the apostolate, etc. It will be easier as a professed. This is real virtue. We must be as "big sisters," "older daughters" of our congregation, holding not continuous assistance but can take responsibilities.

The novitiate is an intense year of prayer, preparation, and study for the consecrated life. It is a rigorous year spent isolated from both the postulants and senior nuns. Except for meals and occasionally in the apostolate, there was no contact with anyone other than with the co-novices. We were not permitted to speak with anyone; before doing so, permission had to be secured from the Mistress of Novices, Sr. Constance. If we ever so much as said one word to anyone, we had to confess this "failure" to the Mistress! During this year, many hours were spent in prayer, and just as many hours were spent in conferences and studies. When we were accepted into the novitiate after approval by the Canonical Visitors, we were given the Constitution, a book containing the rules and regulations of the Daughters of the Holy Word. Every day of novitiate, some part of the study period and/or conference time would be spent not only learning the Constitution, but memorizing it from cover to cover. We were instructed to kiss it each time we picked it up and put it away. This book was considered just as sacred as the Holy Bible (*I thought that this book was venerated much more than the Bible*). We were not permitted to read the Old Testament of the Bible; however, every page of the Constitution of the Order was "devoured!"

During my novitiate from June 30, 1954 to June 30, 1955, I kept copious notes which I would "religiously" review. Excerpts from these are as follows. They demonstrate the brainwashing, allegiance to the will of the superiors, blind obedience and subjugation of self. After years of degradation I took these admonitions seriously, as though they were said only to me.

August 6, 1954 - Form a good character! This does not mean to monopolize the conversation, but to be helpful. When you receive a correction from an equal as well, don't bite back. It is virtue! Those who correct us, love us, and want us to become saints. Therefore, we must love them. Render correcting something easy for the superiors, take all corrections well. Live a good character. It is so beautiful to live in a community!

October 2, 1954. The most obedient are the most intelligent! There is nothing more pleasing to God than to offer back to him the perfect gift he gave us—our will. Imitate Our Lady who after Jesus practices a perfect obedience in everything. Our religious life must be all or nothing.

November 19, 1954. Let us not consider ourselves victims. All the humiliations and corrections we deserve and we deserve more than what we receive.

November 25, 1954 - Thanksgiving. Counsel is a light of the Holy Spirit which enlightens the mind and guides it to right. My child, do nothing without permission. The spirit of independence even comes in the convent, and it enters into the most intimate affairs of our spiritual life and of the necessary things. Our superiors are the interpreters of God's will. There is freedom, yes, but not to dispose of ourselves, but to do God's will. Pleasure cannot be duty. We let ourselves be too much worked up by impressions. One day we are fire, and another day we are down trodden. We must feel a satisfaction when we do our duty, but this duty must not be our pleasure. Counsel must form our conscience into a righteous judgment. We must be guided not by our passions, but by the will of God. God rewards what is done—that is His will, according to His order. This is what our assignment is: to pray for those or for the person that the Lord has put in front of us in authority.

January 28, 1955. Mother Pietra. Pride of mind is hard to correct, and with such pride we don't obey; we have too much self-confidence. There gives birth to impudence's that give way to discord. Do we always obey as religious should? Who doesn't obey; hear that God may take away the grace of our vocation. If there was a little more humility, there would be more love of God, more charity, more happiness. We must always get along with those who are closest to us. To correct pride of the mind, we must subject ourselves just as a child and learn, but with the spirit of prayer and humility. It is not the fact that of the best, but it is to obey. That is the best.

The next two excerpts were from Sr. Constance who knew the berating agenda very well. Because of the great impact they had on me, I was sure to write them. In the first I am accused of gesticulating and being dramatic. After this I noticed both my co-novices and senior nuns were verbose, used their hands, and with both excited and enthusiastic timbers in their voices. I simply was not allowed to be human.

Throwaway Nun

**Rosemary Scirocco-Corsale
Kathleen A. Barreca**

November 28, 1954 - Private conference with Sr. Constance. I am too dramatic. I make too many gestures when I talk. Sr. Constance said that when she sees me make so many gestures, which are theatrical, she would prefer to see me not dressed as a sister. She told me that I never remember anything. She said, "Se/ vuota\ that is, I am empty, I am no one!

January, 1955. During this month I will do my utmost to correct the defects that Sr. Constance stressed, and I should do my apostolate with my head. I want to please Mother Pietra. I don't want to cause her any more sorrow. I caused her enough. I am going to make the practices of piety as she does. I believed my abusers. I degraded myself as they wanted. June 17, 1955. We are obliged to obey always, at all times regardless of who commands, and what the command is. The one and only time we can disobey is when we are commanded to sin. This is impossible. That is, the most serene sister is she who obeys promptly, cheerfully, and blindly without reason or criticism.

Amongst my co-novices, I had been in the convent the longest. One of the novices was a young lady from New Hampshire. She was of Irish descent, with reddish-blonde hair and fair complexion. Both of her parents were schoolteachers, and her oldest brother was in college. From the beginning, it was made known that she was being groomed to attend college, translate books, write books, and be an intellect in the Order. As a result, she was afforded special privileges almost from the date of her entrance into the convent. She never worked at any machine, and rarely came into the apostolate. She spent her time doing "intellectual" things; she spent her days studying, reading, writing, and learning the Italian language, so that she would be able to translate. She never did any form of manual labor. In fact, this special treatment caused her co-novices to call

Throwaway Nun

Rosemary Scirocco-Corsale
Kathleen A. Barreca

her "Sister Special." She knew what our nickname for her was, but she did not seem to mind. She is the only co-novice with whom I had very little dealings because I knew her to be handpicked by Mother Pietra and Sr. Constance. I knew her to be one of their "spies." After novitiate, she continued her college education and completed her Doctorate.

Another of my co-novices was from Ohio, just a few miles from my parents' home. She was the youngest novice and was already a full-fledged nun. She was the youngest of our group, as well. She always struggled between wanting to stay in the convent and wanting to leave. As enticements to remain in the convent, Mother Pietra and her cohorts protected her, in a sense. They watched over her, taught her to operate the linotype machine, and spared her from the hard, manual labor. However, none of this seemed to impress her. Unlike "Sister Special," she never made herself to appear better than anyone else. Because of her many inner conflicts, she always had difficulty eating. Sometimes there would be days that she could not eat at all. According to the rules, one had to sit at the table and finish whatever was on her plate, even if it took all night! My heart went out to her; I knew what it meant to be humiliated and degraded. I would make deliberate efforts to pass by her chair or even to sit next to her at mealtime. I would sneak food off her plate and gobble it down before anyone could see me. I would put her bread in my pocket and eat it in the dark of night or in the bathroom. So many times, she would thank me, privately. If I were around, she would have less fear because she knew I would come to her aid. To this day, we remain close friends. Her difficulty with food is long gone.

Every novice, including myself, had her own idiosyncrasies; but none of them ever tried to berate me on purpose. Once we were at the

Throwaway Nun

**Rosemary Scirocco-Corsale
Kathleen A. Barreca**

dinner table and I asked Sr. Constance for a new bar of soap. Sr. Agatha mentioned that she still had her soap, and that she also had been using it to wash her hair. The Mistress eagerly took this opportunity to publicly berate and humiliate me. She went on and on about how incapable I was and how I would never learn anything about the vow of poverty because I was unable to conserve and use things in a timely manner. She reasoned that if Sr. Agatha's soap had lasted this long, then mine should have also lasted if I had not been so wasteful. I said nothing. I had learned so very long ago to accept whatever they said to me. Later that evening when the novices were doing some cleaning in the chapel, Sr. Agatha came to me. No one was near us; most of all we were hidden from view. She apologized profusely. She kept saying that she was sorry. She said she did not have the slightest inkling that Sr. Constance would take her statement and twist it to use in such a humiliating fashion. I assured her that all was fine and that there was no need for her to be upset over the matter. Nonetheless, I recognized the modus operandi well; it was one played over and over again by all the co-novices during that year. It had happened during my postulancy, and I saw it happening among several of the senior nuns. After I would be publicly tongue lashed and degraded, I would get these private apologies. No one had the intestinal fortitude to stand by me, take my position, or defend me. The secret admissions of regret or sadness were never spoken in the presence of Mother Pietra or her spies. To do so would be to run the risk of placing themselves in the position of becoming a scapegoat. They, too, contributed to the perpetuation of the abuse upon me; better me than they, better the "stupid one" than to incur Mother Pietra's wrath. It was better that these horrific public humiliations occur to someone who would just accept it all without flinching a muscle or so

Throwaway Nun

Rosemary Scirocco-Corsale
Kathleen A. Barreca

much as to utter a sigh than to expose themselves as being sympathetic. So much for their Christian spirit of justice and righteousness; so much for truth!

It was the task assigned to the novices that during that year we would be responsible for the chapel. We would clean, sweep, scrub, and run the vacuum weekly. We would take turns changing the altar linens. Special handmade tatted or sequined borders would be hung under the linen altar cloth. For Holy Days, there would be fresh flowers. Since the Mass was spoken in Latin at that time, there were plaques in the center and on both sides of the altar to help the celebrating priest to remember all of the Latin. On weekdays and Sundays, these plaques were simply framed ones, but for the holidays they were very ornate plaques. These were of Gothic style with gilded frames and thin spires. On this particular occasion, it was my turn to dress the altar. I carefully removed the plaques from the cupboard and laid them on the altar. Unfortunately, my sleeve got caught on one of the spires, causing the plaque to go tumbling to the floor. No damage occurred to the gilded frame, but the glass cracked. I immediately went to Sr. Constance to consign myself; that is, to confess what had happened. She went to the chapel to survey the damage. When she exited, I received a severe tongue-lashing. She accused me of being distracted, careless, and stupid. Following this barrage, she solemnly announced that I was never to work in the chapel with my co-novices again; I never did, until a couple of months before I left. When the other novices were cleaning and preparing the chapel, I would be assigned other tasks like scrubbing or sweeping the floors of other rooms, or other manual labor. My heart and stomach sank to the soles of my feet. It was considered a privilege to clean and prepare the chapel for liturgies. To be denied this participation was a deep feeling of loss. I felt that this was a deliberate effort to keep me from closeness with God whom we believed to be present in the "Tabernacle" of the chapel.

During the early winter months of 1954, there was a general cleaning of the chapel. Special oils and waxes were used to clean and polish the walls which were paneled with mahogany wood. I was assigned to work in the chapel but only to do the scrubbing and heavy work. All the statues had been taken off their pedestals and placed in the dining hall. The statue of Jesus had been set near the open archway leading into the room. During the course of cleaning, this life-sized statue was passed by everyone many times. Once, when I had again passed the statue, I made an off-the-cuff remark which was not meant to be malicious; I stated that I was as tall as the statue. At that very moment Sr. Constance was coming down the stairs and heard the remark. Again, she blasted me before my co-novices. She wanted to know how I could dare to imagine that I was a big as the Lord. She repeatedly said I was a nobody, a nothing, unable to do the simplest of tasks compared to the Lord who was a worker of miracles, a perfect person, not the stupid, distracted novice that I was. She proceeded to mourn that what I had just done was blasphemy, that I needed to confess this horrible sin, and that I was in great danger of losing my soul! The tongue-lashing I took without rebuttal; however, I was seized with terror lest I should die that very night and lose my soul to the devil! I had not meant to scandalize anyone by what I thought was so innocent a passing remark. Immediately, I silently began to ask the Lord's pardon, to seek forgiveness, and to beg for mercy. I begged the Lord to let me live until I went to Confession. I asked pardon of my co-novices present, because I did not want to give them a bad example. None of them

Throwaway Nun

Rosemary Scirocco-Corsale
Kathleen A. Barreca

made any comment. The incident was never mentioned again. The agony of losing my soul to the devil, that I could have blasphemed, and that I might die, remained with me. This is another example of how I was constantly accused of being a bad example to those younger than myself. During the novitiate year, Sr. Constance never missed an opportunity to degrade me publicly or in private.

During each monthly retreat, we had a private conference with the Mistress of Novices. After seven years, I had come to dread these times. For me they were occasions to sit and to listen while I was humiliated and debased. What Sr. Constance kept insisting were grave failures on my part, were in fact petty things. I was taken to task for those few times she noticed my feet were not close together, when my eyes were not cast down, when my shoulders were not straight, or when she did not think I sat down gracefully enough. The list went on and on. Life continued in this fashion for the entire year. Each time that these degrading would take place, I would be overcome with waves of fear and depression. I feared that I would be sent out of the convent. I felt that to lose my vocation was to lose my soul. I feared that no matter how hard I tried, I could never change enough to please my superiors. I feared that I was a failure in the eyes of our Lord and that I could never deserve to become His "bride." Sr. Constance had said to the group, "The superiors have the power to send a temporary professed away, and not renew the vows for just reasons. And, one of these reasons is not to live with the religious spirit. It is necessary to seek God in our superiors." And, I believed that they would use the full power of their authority to cast me from their midst.

I learned well how to degrade myself. All these very negative humiliations, feelings, and emotions caused me to be more depressed.

Throwaway Nun

Rosemary Scirocco-Corsale
Kathleen A. Barreca

Notwithstanding this oppression, I dared not show any emotions on the outside. I had been scolded over and over again in Staten Island for showing reactions on my face. I learned to become "blank." However, my physical being was beginning to demonstrate the effects of these negative pressures. Shortly after receiving my habit, I developed a small rash behind both my ears. At first, the rash would flare up and, with no care, would go away. During the early months of novitiate, the rash was to return with a vengeance. It worsened and got redder and larger. My ears would become itchy and scabbed. If I dared scratch them, the scabs would open and the rash would ooze a yellow-colored fluid. I would wipe this fluid with my handkerchief and hold it on the rash until it would stop oozing. When I finally told Sr. Constance about the rash, I was given a small jar of Vaseline to use. I used the ointment faithfully, but the problem persisted. It never got any better. At this time, Sr. Constance said this (June, 1955), "As regards our health, simply obey. Do as the superiors say. God will bless you with health. Do not do as the doctor says." This admonition would haunt my days and nights in a short time.

While we were in novitiate, Mother Pietra had the idea that Jesus would particularly bless the novices if they were to go out selling books. We were supposed to make more money than the senior nuns. This would be the temporal sign that God was showing His favor. So, we were sent out in the City of Buffalo to sell books. I was paired with Sr. Maria. The day was wonderful for me! Sr. Maria was easy-going as well as energetic. Selling books was not one of the things she wanted to do. She had been taught how to operate the printing presses while we were still postulants and she really liked to do that. We talked about what would be in store for us after we had finished our novitiate. I did not tell her that I doubted that I would finish the year because of how negatively Sr. Constance treated me. Almost prophetically, I told her that if I succeeded in completing novitiate that I would be sent back to Staten Island "to work hard." Sr. Maria never responded. We continued to go from door to door. The people were especially kind and generous. Did they notice that we were so young? Did they act this way because we looked like a couple of kids? Did they buy books from us because they "pitied" us for being so youthful looking? Whatever the reason, Sr. Maria and I had a very successful day. We returned back to the convent with empty satchels. This appears to have also been the case with the other novices. Sr. Constance and Mother Pietra reported to us that our "propaganda" had been very fruitful. They were talking about money. We were never told how much money we actually brought back to the convent that day; we were never sent out again. It seems that Rome somehow learned of our being sent out and the practice was stopped before it began. During the novitiate, there was to be no contact with the outside world, no going out to sell books and asking for donations, no interruption of the purpose and goal of the special year. It was decided that our going out "into the world" would cause serious distractions and loss of focus by the novices toward the intense prayer life, study of their constitution, the congregation, and constant examination of one's vocation.

Shortly after I entered the novitiate year, my sister, who wrote to me regularly, informed me that she was expecting their first child. She and her husband were very elated; they had been married for four years and their early efforts at trying to start a family had been unsuccessful. In the middle of March, 1955, she wrote me to tell me the good news! Sr. Constance handed me her letter before starting our dinner. I was anxious

Throwaway Nun

Rosemary Scirocco-Corsale
Kathleen A. Barreca

to read it, but put it in my pocket because I wanted to offer this small waiting period to the Lord for the health of both my sister and the new baby. My co-novices knew that I had been expecting the news and they seemed just as anxious as I was. Several asked when I would read the letter. Even Sr. Constance appeared condescending and somewhat looking forward to the news. In fact, the novices stayed at the table after the senior nuns and postulants had left the dining hall. I learned that my sister had given birth to a little girl; her name was Kathleen Ann. She was my first niece, the first grandchild for my parents. This was such a memorable occasion because everyone showed great kindness and happiness at the news. It was one of the rare times that Sr. Constance nodded in approval and smiled.

If Mother Pietra and Sr. Constance expected great blessings and special graces to be granted to the Order during our novitiate, it did not take long for the fruits to ripen. We were informed that Mother Pietra had met with the Archbishop of a large Eastern diocese and that the Daughters of the Holy Word would soon begin to build their first custom-made Motherhouse. It would be built on the border of a well-known city and was to become the United States headquarters for the Order, and it still is. I had a very special reason to be happy. In the early summer of 1953, the nuns opened the new convent, and I was ordered to go and help establish the new "house." I was ecstatic; it was considered a privilege and source of personal blessing from God to do so. So, I went east. Even for my lack of sophistication, immaturity, and stupidity, what I saw was very disturbing. Mother Pietra had selected a second-story apartment in the center of a street lined with very old New England townhouses. They had been poorly maintained, looked dilapidated, and seemed not to have had

Throwaway Nun

Rosemary Scirocco-Corsale
Kathleen A. Barreca

any exterior paint on them for decades. The street was well known as the "red-light district." It seems that some charitable Catholic had offered this site to the Bishop for the "new nuns." I doubt that the Bishop knew the situation. However, what was most distressing was the musty, dusty odor that pervaded everything. The windows were actually gray and no sunlight came through them because of the grime. There was an oriental-type carpet in the living room which was so worn, the design and colors were barely visible. The kitchen was dirty with greasy walls and cupboards, dirty floors, and an even dirtier cooking stove. The day after my arrival, I was told the reason why I had been sent to this new "house;" my job was to scrub and clean the three bedroom apartment. It was my job to get rid of the grease, grime, dirt, and terrible smell. I was to start with the kitchen. So, each day the four other nuns would leave in the early morning to work in the new book center, and I was to remain there alone and work. I scrubbed and cleaned; I cleaned and scrubbed. My fingers had become raw from cleaning the kitchen stove. In two days, the kitchen sparkled. I had washed the walls and they looked brighter. I began in the bedroom and the planks began to show the grain. I waxed them and they looked good. I took the Oriental run outside to the rear of the townhouse. I had to walk down a dark, drafty corridor to get to the small yard. The grass was brown and thatched from lack of care. Three lengths of rope had been strung from one side to the other of the small enclosure. I threw the foul carpet over one of the lines. With the handle of the broom, I beat the carpet. The first several blows produced billows of gray dirt and dust. I was covered in gray, but I persisted. When I could see no more dirt fall from the carpet, I rolled it up and carried it to the apartment. The small grassy area was totally covered with dirt and looked gray. I didn't know

Throwaway Nun

**Rosemary Scirocco-Corsale
Kathleen A. Barreca**

how to solve this problem; I prayed that the senior nuns would not come to find out. After scrubbing the floor several times, I laid the carpet down (the carpet had not become more colorful, but it was evident that it was much cleaner).

The habit I wore was becoming dirtier with each passing day. I wore this habit to do all the cleaning. On Sunday, I donned my Sunday clothes to go to church. I had several windows to clean before hanging the curtains. In those days, we cleaned windows with a popular glass cleaner that was bright pink and thick, like pudding. It did a good job of removing the decades of grime which had accumulated on the glass panes. I had already washed all the woodwork around the windows, and I had to hang outside of each window to clean the outside. On the inside, I had to use a ladder because the windows were high and once, when I was moving the ladder to another window, the bottle of glass cleaner fell and spilled all over the left side of my veil. I cleaned off the excess, but I was quite a sight. I proceeded to the first floor to clean the window in the front door. The door leading to the second floor apartment closed....and locked! I had no key. I looked a sight. There was no telephone available to call the bookstore to have one of the nuns come with the key to let me back into the apartment. I prayed and asked the Lord for help in resolving the problem. I knew that it was between 12 noon and 12:30 p.m. because I had just finished eating my lunch. I went to the house next door and an older man answered the door. He was either leery at the spectacle before him, or he was naturally cautious because of where he lived. He only opened the door enough for one eye to look out. I quickly explained my problem and asked if he would kindly call the Fire Department. I pleaded with him to tell the firefighters not to sound the sirens. He nodded and closed the door,

Throwaway Nun

Rosemary Scirocco-Corsale
Kathleen A. Barreca

and I slipped back next door hoping that no one was looking out of their windows. I waited; the thought passed through my mind that maybe the man would not make the phone call. I can still remember the incredulous looks on their faces as each fireman came through the door. They were very kind and soon had the door opened. I thanked them and sent them on their way with God's blessings. I am sure that this was one call that they talked about for weeks thereafter. So, when all the scrubbing, cleaning, sweeping, washing, scraping, and polishing had been done, I was promptly sent back to Staten Island. I was disappointed; I was not to help establish the new convent, I had been sent only to do the dirty and heavy work. So, in secret, I offered my labors and heavy heart to the Lord for the success of this new convent.

Therefore, when we learned that this would be the city where the Daughters of the Holy Word would build the new, large Motherhouse, I secretly thanked God that He was good enough to show me that my toil was not in vain.

Notwithstanding the intimacy, isolation, and intensity of the year of novitiate, I continued to remain very private about my true inner self. I did not share with anyone my thoughts, emotions, feelings, opinions, and least of all, my desires. I talked about personal things and issues that were common knowledge, or rehashed my many reprimands with Sr. Constance. There were enough public humiliations and debasements which gave her more than grist for the mill during those monthly conferences. I continued to keep my interior self-hidden. I never told her about any internal reactions I had toward the degrading, the public humiliations, and the negative atmosphere I felt I was subjected to every day. I dared not show any initiative or intelligence. I never shared with her, or with anyone else, my deepened spiritual journey. These things I kept locked inside myself, and I would enter that "inner space" that I had created for myself to process everything. My prayer life seemed to take on a new form. I found myself having long conversations with Jesus, the Divine Master, and His Blessed Mother. More and more, I turned to her to ask her for help and protection. I truly felt that she was my "spiritual Mother" in whom I could take refuge when I felt buffeted from all sides. I had no trouble praying, and I had no difficulties with my interior-spiritual growth—I just never shared these with anyone. I had learned my lessons well from the past. I tried hard not to be obvious about keeping my interior self-hidden. I am not sure if Sr. Constance had any insight into my reticence. More than once, I was struck with waves of fear of being discovered and of losing my vocation to religious life. During this year, both Mother Pietra and Sr. Constance repeated over and over again during their conferences with the novices that we were to be open with the superiors. We were to tell them everything, barring nothing. Following are notes that I wrote after my monthly conferences with one or the other of them, as well as some personal thoughts:

June, 1954 - "Confide all in your superiors. Tell them all of your inclinations and affections, open your heart to them and you can't go wrong. Tell everything to the superiors, all of your tendencies, all temptations, difficulties, the condition of your health, and of your families."

August, 1954 - "Those who correct us love us and want us to become saints. Therefore, we must love them. Render correcting something easy for the superior. Take all corrections well. Obedience is giving up our will to do the will of God, which is manifested through the lawful superior. Obey always." October, 1954 - (Sr. Constance) "The superior doesn't look either at me or my talents or what I like or don't like, but at the necessities of the congregation. All the rest is secondary. Our superiors look at what we are best capable of doing and for what we are prepared to do."

November, 1954 - "Our superiors are the interpreters of God's will. There is freedom, yes, but not to dispose of ourselves but to do God's will. To tell all and to put ourselves into the hands of those who guide us; it is with this opening up of ourselves that we do not make a mistake. Dispose ourselves to receive the counsel given and pray to follow it. Never expect the superior to see your side of the story."

November, 1954 - (Mother Pietra) "Trust your superior—never rash judge the superior."

December 4, 1954 - (Sr. Constance) "Have the best disposition when the superior corrects your defects and don't get any long face.

December 17, 1954 - (Mother Pietra) "Whenever we must consign ourselves, do so with simplicity. Do not be afraid, even when we get scolded we deserve it. Be careful; if we are careful, we do not have to be afraid."

December 18, 1954 - (Mother Pietra) "Always stay with the superior. Who is with the superior, is with God. Have no particular friendships. Be open and sincere with superiors."

January, 1955 - (Mother Pietra) "How can we please God if we don't please our superiors? Get it straight! If we please our superior, we are sure to please God. Ask the superior for everything—permissions, work, etc. Be more to ourselves and to Sr. Constance."

Throwaway Nun

Rosemary Scirocco-Corsale
Kathleen A. Barreca

January 10, 1955 - (Sr. Constance) "True humility is truth, and we do not shrink when our superiors or our own sisters correct us."

January 22, 1955 - (Mother Pietra) "Those who are afraid of the superior are those who don't do well. It shows we are proud and that we don't want to be corrected. Even as professed, the superior can send us home just the same. Obey—do what the superior says. Correct your million defects now! The superiors expect you to change now during these remaining months of the novitiate. Remain faithful to what you are told by the superiors. The local superior has the graces for us. Those who obey the local superiors are the best nuns. You can fool man, but not God."

January 28, 1955 - (Mother Pietra) "Whenever we have something, go to the superior. Be in a position for good information so that they may send you with anyone, anywhere, and so that the superior can be sure that you will be a good representative for the congregation."

February, 1955 - (Sr. Constance) "Take counsel from whom the Lord has put at our side to guide us. The prudent man seeks advice. Stay close to your superiors. Don't see the person to obey, but the image of God, because she represents God in our midst."

February, 1955 - (Mother Pietra) "Death rather than to be a 67c millstone to the arch 1, 1955 - (Sr. Constance) "Therefore, it is so necessary to see God in our superiors. Obedience is a supernatural moral virtue which inclines us to submit our will to that of our lawful superiors, insofar as they are the representatives of God. Obedience is better than sacrifice."

March 11, 1955 - (Mother Pietra) "Form a good character, but really well. We have to start the congregation here in the United States. If you don't have a good character, the superiors can't send us here or there as they wish."

March 20, 1955 - (Sr. Constance) "A certain sister is rebellious to the superior because she did not obey in the small things. When you are ordered by the superiors to do anything, look at her, answer saying something to assure her you've understood."

April 19, 1955 - (Mother Pietra) "When we think we know more than the superiors, we do not even have a basic education. We don't obey the superiors because she is good and holy, but because by her office she represents God for us and manifests His will to us. The superior must be obeyed. The subject must obey the superior for the love of God, and thus humility will be exercised."

May 6, 1955 - (Private conference with Sr. Constance) "Be humble and let yourself be corrected, and ask for corrections. Never feel offended when a senior nun corrects you, and do not take this as a victim. Otherwise, we lose the merits. Furthermore, corrections are not to be taken as a victim; there's no need for it. If we want progress, then we should want to be corrected. It is hard to see our own defects. We must have the right idea; that is, to correct our defects. But, in order to correct them, we first have to know what they are. Hence, it is important that someone else tells us what our faults are, since we are so easy to excuse ourselves. Our true friends are those who tell us our defects. It is better to clean up the sore spots here on earth, so we can go straight to heaven."

May 28, 1955 - (Mother Pietra) "Put in practice the advices given you. Put in practice the little things; it is so important to do small things. Obey the local superior. Don't say 'in novitiate they told us to do our say this or that.' No, do what you are told, always."

Throwaway Nun

Rosemary Scirocco-Corsale
Kathleen A. Barreca

Openness with our superiors was expected; had they sensed my reluctance to open my guts to them? On the horns of this dilemma, I had to make a decision. If I opened my interior life to them, I would be even more ridiculed and debased, such as had just happened when I tried to trust Sr. Clara in Staten Island. If I chose to remain hidden, I might be found out and promptly sent home for whatever sins, failures, and faults that Sr. Constance and Mother Pietra might report to my parents and the other nuns. I prayed for guidance in this matter. I chose to remain with my hidden, inner self. I chose to shut out the pathway for future recriminations upon my head, giving the superiors no access to the very recesses of my heart. In the end, I chose well.

By the middle of May, 1955, I had not yet been banished from the convent as I had thought in the beginning of the novitiate. There was never any mention of my leaving even though I agonized almost daily. In fact, Sr. Constance informed me and my other co-novices that we were to make final preparations for the profession of the vows of chastity, poverty, and obedience, and for the changing of our names. The vows were to close out the last chapter of any association with the "outside" world, and the name change was to announce to ourselves and to others that we were now the "brides" of Christ, Himself! All during the month of May, we made great preparations, starting with our monthly retreats. There were many conferences throughout the year; however, during the last months of our novitiate, it seemed that Mother Pietra led more of these conferences than at any other time. The thrust of these conferences was the unlimited and unrequited rendering of obedience in all things. The previous excerpts of these conferences demonstrate an almost fanatical approach to the practice of the vow of obedience. Some admonitions were ominous and made a great impression on me. I had been browbeaten for the last eight years and had become so good at debasing myself; I took these advices and admonitions to heart. I could not help but feel that they were telling those things specifically for me. I considered the profession of vows to be so serious and momentous for me that I actually could not sleep at night and would pray until I was too tired to continue.

As part of the preparation for the profession, the novices were summoned to their sleeping quarters and were required to take all of the boxes of our personal belongings into the corridor. Sr. Constance had placed a large box in the center and told us that we were to place all items of worth and value into it. They were to go to the Order; everything else was to be thrown away. A nun who professes the vow of poverty can own nothing, possess nothing, and can have nothing which might provoke worldly attachment. So, into the box I placed a set of sheets and pillow cases, two bath towels, and two washcloths which were sent to me by my parents. I gave Sr. Constance a silver dollar which my parents had given me a few years previously. Into the trash box I placed all my school notebooks, letters from home; birthday, Christmas, and Easter cards from my family; small mementos from our 1948 visit to the New York Museum, and other pieces of paper amongst which were a couple of drawings. The most heartbreaking thing I threw away was the red rose I had taken from my sister's coffin two years earlier. It was dried, but the deep burgundy color remained. I held the rose to my breast and then cast it away. I made sure no one saw the tears rolling down my cheeks. And so within an hour, we had managed to cast aside any vestige of "attachment" to our past lives. We were "free" of the world and anything in it. This

Throwaway Nun

Rosemary Scirocco-Corsale
Kathleen A. Barreca

event might have passed, as so many others did, without any special meaning to me had it not been for the red rose.

Sr. Constance had informed the group of novices that during the monthly retreat in June we would each have a "private conference" with Mother Pietra. When she had said this, I felt my heart jump in my chest! These monthly conferences had become torturous for me. I was browbeaten, humiliated, and debased during those few I had had with her in the past; I had no reason to think any differently this time. In fact, I worried that Mother Pietra and Sr. Constance had plotted a special torture for me—I thought that during this conference, Mother Pietra would solemnly announce that I would not make profession and that I would either remain a little sister for a year or more, or be sent back to my parents' home! My fears increased hourly during the day as I observed my co-novices going to or returning from their private conferences. I had still not been called when the bell rang for our evening prayers which preceded our retiring. My heart was beating so quickly; I could feel it in my throat. I want to cry out, but I held everything in. I could feel my stomach tighten as though it were in a vise. I felt like I needed to vomit, but I knew that to do so would be to incur the displeasure and added wrath of my superiors. As we lined up for the walk to our dormitories, it seemed that my heart had fallen to the very soles of my feet. Then, I heard Sr. Constance call my name, and tell me to wait for Mother Pietra. My stomach tightened even more. Mother Pietra descended the stairs and came toward me. I could not "read' her facial expression. She guided me outside and we walked toward the novices' sleeping quarters. I could hardly believe my eyes; I could hardly believe what I was hearing! For the first time in eight years, she did not humiliate or degrade me. She was motherly in her admonitions,

Throwaway Nun

Rosemary Scirocco-Corsale
Kathleen A. Barreca

advising that now I would be a true professed nun and that I needed to follow the Constitution of the Order and become a true saint. She pointed out my failings, e.g. talking less, taking corrections well, becoming less distracted. However, she said these things not in her usual harsh voice and expressions that always let me know her absolute disapproval of me. She discussed my profession of vows. I was so elated at this turn of events that I felt like leaping into the air and proclaiming to the entire world that I had, at last, pleased the superiors! I dared not react; I dared not make even one comment except the occasional nod of the head, yes or no. I was so afraid of any display of emotion or feeling. I was afraid that to share my elation would be to bring the negatives down upon my head. I showed heroic restraint and I chose well. For the first time in eight years, Mother Pietra had actually touched my forehead to make the sign of the Cross. For the first time in eight years, she patted my forehead with her fist. After these horrible and painful years, no one would fault me for experiencing such joy! I just knew that my life's fortunes were about to change for the better. I just knew that my profession day would be magical, joyful, and filled with mercy and blessings from my "Bridegroom." I was ready to take my vows; I was ready to become a full-fledged nun; I was ready to be a Daughter of St. Paul. After this fantastic, private conference, I went to bed and fell asleep immediately. I slept like a baby! For days I could feel this inner elation and inner joy. It was unbelievable that I would have become pleasing to my superiors; that they could, finally, find some redeeming values in me! And so, I passed all the examinations and written tests for profession; I had received acceptance into the Order from Rome!

We knew that we would be having an eight-day spiritual retreat just before our profession. This retreat, following the method of St.

Throwaway Nun

**Rosemary Scirocco-Corsale
Kathleen A. Barreca**

Ignatius, was intense and rigorous. The retreat would end one day before our profession. Father Bamo would be our retreat master. So one evening in the conference room just before the retreat, Sr. Constance said that we were to make a list of faults and defects of each of our co-novices. These lists were to be given to her, and we were instructed not to discuss them with each other. A week later during the conference, Sr. Constance handed each novice their particular list of faults and defects prepared by her peers. When she came to my desk, she said that it was to be expected that I would get the longest list and would have the worst defects listed. I crumbled and seemed to melt into my seat. I could barely believe that my co-novices would degrade me in this manner, especially when each of them—except Sr. Special—at one time or another had come privately to me to tell me how sorry they felt because of the terrible way I was being treated. I can clearly remember how hard it had been for me to find faults with them. As I read the list, I was simply thunderstruck! The list looked so long because there were much duplication, but Sr. Constance had not mentioned that fact. So many of these faults, and defects were only things that they had heard the superiors blast me about, over and over again. I can never recall any of my co-novices discussing these issues over the past year. I was deeply hurt; I felt betrayed by them. And the more I reviewed the list, the pettier and out of place the comments seemed. I still have the list of my 42 faults that came from my five co-novices; after eliminating the repetitions, the following fourteen faults remain:

- laughs too loudly
- puts hands on hips
- too many gestures (talks with hands)
- scratches her ears

Throwaway Nun

Rosemary Scirocco-Corsale
Kathleen A. Barreca

- bad posture
- shows distraction
- too showy in her devotions
- goes from one extreme to another when corrected
- walks heavily
- always misunderstands
- sits with her legs apart
- rather sarcastic
- wobbles when she runs
- acts as a superior

Once this list was given to each of us, it was never mentioned or discussed again. I never had another private conference with Sr. Constance, so there never was a discussion of the list with her. I never shared this list with any of my future superiors.

On June 30, 1955, we seven made our formal profession of vows. The Lake Erie side of the manse in Derby had been decorated with a portable altar, white drapes, and a kneeling bench covered with satin fabric and ornamented with fresh sprigs of fern and roses. The lawn had been prepared with special seats for us; behind our seats were folding chairs for our families, relatives, and friends. Present were other religious, both nuns and priests from other congregations. Benefactors and friends of the Order had also gathered for the occasion. My family had come from Ohio. My parents were so pleased. (*I saw my three-month-old niece, Kathleen Ann, for the first time. She was a beautiful baby.*) Each novice knelt before the celebrant priest and pronounced her intention to enter the congregation of the Daughters of St. Paul professed her vows of chastity,

Throwaway Nun

Rosemary Scirocco-Corsale
Kathleen A. Barreca

poverty, and obedience, and received her new name. When my turn had come, I repeated this prayer:

"I, Sister Rosemary, in honor of the Most Holy Trinity, of the Immaculate Virgin Mary, Queen of Heaven, and of the Divine Master, for my own greater sanctification and that of my neighbor, with the help of the Divine Grace, offer, give, consecrate myself entirely to God, and in your hands, Superior, make the vows of obedience, chastity, and poverty in the society of the Daughters of St. Paul. According to the Constitution of the same Society, so help me God. Amen."

After pronouncing of vows, Mother Pietra placed a missionary crucifix which hung from a black, silk cord, over our hearts. She then placed a special pin on the left of our habits. Finally, we stood and were given our new names. "Henceforth," the priest said to me, "you will be called 'Sister Mary Carmel'". I was given the name of my sister who had died two years earlier. I could hear a sob escape from my mother; I had not told my family what my new name would be. The novices had been informed of the names during the retreat prior to profession. I would bear my sister's name, and I was pleased! I would carry the name of our Heavenly Mother forever.

After the ceremony, each novice was permitted to spend the remainder of the day with her family and loved ones, to eat with them, and to visit the apostolate and other areas of the property. Very soon the day ended and our families began to depart. Most had traveled hundreds of miles, and night was going to fall soon. My family was going to return to Ohio that very night, the day had indeed been glorious! I was so happy; I thought my heart would burst! Finally, I was a full-fledged nun. Finally, I had become "married to Jesus, Himself." The Blessed Virgin Mary was

Throwaway Nun   **Rosemary Scirocco-Corsale**
                                                                                  Kathleen A. Barreca

my "celestial Mother-in law." I felt like the luckiest woman in the world. No day in my life could ever compare to this; not even the day when I received my habit was this wondrous! It seemed that I could actually feel Jesus put His arms around me and kiss my cheek. Oh, how I wanted to hold on to the feelings and emotions of this day! How much I wanted to hold on to the peace of this day! I could not imagine even heaven to be more joyous!

      Within two weeks of my profession, I was ordered to return to Staten Island. All during my novitiate, I had prayed that I would be assigned to a smaller convent other than Staten Island. I had such a sense of doom and foreboding about returning there. In fact, I remember that in the first months of our novitiate I had gone out selling books in Buffalo with Sr. Maria. I told her then that I felt that after profession I would be sent back to Staten Island to "work hard;" I had made a prophetic statement! Even though my heart was heavy, I obeyed. And so, I had gone full circle in my religious life: I had entered the convent in Staten Island in 1947 when I was just 13 years old, and here I was in July, 1955, back in Staten Island as a full professed nun. I was twenty-one years old, and I had been in the convent for eight years.

Throwaway Nun

Rosemary Scirocco-Corsale
Kathleen A. Barreca

PART FOUR

So, less than a month after my religious profession of vows, I was sent to the convent in Staten Island, New York. My other co-novices stayed in the motherhouse in Derby for several months before receiving their assignments. Within the recesses of my soul I had hoped that I would be sent to another convent, but I understood that my assignment to Staten Island meant the utilization of my physical strength and stamina for hard labor.

Just days after arriving in New York State I wrote: I am again in New York, it's my place for another year to work and pray and progress. Put away the past, the failures and look into the future and live well the present. It is so important! Put into practice your resolutions and all will be well within and without. In moments of discouragement and vexation, look deep into your heart for consolation from Christ; there He reigns as king. Thus, there won't be any serious regrets.

On the other hand, Staten Island had been a very painful three years before my novitiate. Now, I hoped, that my profession and entering the ranks of the other sisters there would make me less of a target and more acceptable. If they had stopped calling me the unkind names after I had received my habit, I reasoned, and then perhaps they would accept me as one of them. How wrong could I have been?

For the first few months I experienced no problems, no humiliations or confrontations. I knew my place and I did as I was told....always. I understood that I was to use my physical strength in every way possible, whenever and wherever told to do so. Very shortly this hiatus would come to an abrupt end.

Throwaway Nun

Rosemary Scirocco-Corsale
Kathleen A. Barreca

Soon after my arrival, I was put in charge of keeping the cellar clean, stacking the books and pamphlets on the shelves for the nuns to place in their bags for daily sales trips, and mailing out requests for various religious books. In addition, I was assigned to clean the third floor bathrooms, hallway, and stairs down to the first floor. I was to clean the tiled corridor on the first floor, and clean the parlor, which was the visitor's room, once a week. Later, I was ordered to clean the bathroom on the second floor, also. It had white tile flooring, a white pedestal sink, a white claw-footed bathtub, and a standard white commode. The floor had to be washed almost every day.

It became apparent that all of the menial jobs had been given to me. I was the "youngest" of the nuns and, therefore, subservient to them all. Together with all of the above duties, I was paired with a senior nun to go out every day to sell books and pamphlets, request donations, and ask for any goods the senior sister told me were needed. My days were long and laborious. I had no time for rest or recreation, except for those few occasions when we all rested or during high holy days or patron saint days. My additional responsibilities in the cellar did not leave me much spare time. However, the convent in Staten Island was known for everyone working very hard, especially going out every day and bringing back hundreds of dollars from donations and proceeds of book selling. Each senior sister had a "territory" in the greater New York City and New Jersey areas. These were areas which the senior sister would go to every month or every few months. Within these territories were major contributors who would become "benefactors" and give large financial contributions every few months, twice a year, or once annually. These benefactors were generally businessmen who also contributed goods and

Throwaway Nun

Rosemary Scirocco-Corsale
Kathleen A. Barreca

supplies which were sent to Rome after being crated in large, wooden boxes. It was also my job to go to the garage and steel strap those boxes after they had been nailed shut.

During my novitiate, Sr. Clara had been sent to another convent where she remained the superior. Now Sr. Jerald was the superior in New York. In all my years of religious life I knew her to be obedient and very devoted to Mother Pietra. I also thought of her as a very devout nun. Through the years she had been kind to me and never caused me any grief. However, the next two years would prove I was painfully mistaken.

Shortly after Christmas, 1955, the peace was to be broken. I began the New Year, 1956, in great inner turmoil. During the conference held with the superior on our monthly retreat, Sr. Jerald accused me of acting and imitating Sr. Mary of the Holy Innocents. She further went on to tell me that this "bad influence" was the result of my lack of dedication to the congregation and of my lassitude. Needless to say, I was devastated. Everyone knew that Sr. Mary of the Innocents was a nonconformist who questioned the authority of Mother Pietra and flaunted her objections in front of everyone! When she was refused permission to learn to drive a car, she found someone in the area where she went to sell books to teach her. In the 1950's, there was a great influx in the New York City area of Puerto Rican people, and she wanted to be able to communicate with them in their language. So, when she was refused permission to learn the Spanish language, she got a book to learn for herself. When Mother Pietra would require that more money be brought in from books sales and donations, Sr. Mary showed little concern. She did not venerate Mother Pietra, nor did she kiss her hand or try to get "close" to her. It was common knowledge that this fierce dislike was a two-way street. Sr. Mary

Throwaway Nun

Rosemary Scirocco-Corsale
Kathleen A. Barreca

of the Holy Innocents threatened Mother Pietra's authority and the ways she dominated the American Province of the Holy Word Order. Therefore, when Sr. Jerald accused me of acting and being like Sr. Mary, I was taken aback. I had never behaved in a recalcitrant way. I had never questioned Mother Pietra's authority or the manner in which she used fear to dominate the nuns in the American Province. I never refused to obey orders, nor tried to do anything without permission. So, the accusations caused my inner peace to be shattered. It caused upheaval within me. I knew that this was the beginning of much turmoil. And, I was right!

As each monthly retreat came and went, I was upbraided for this or that, usually for being disobedient; following the actions of those nuns who were not the best examples, and of talking too much. These accusations and upbraiding happened so often that I was beside myself and at a total loss. The struggle in my heart and soul had begun. This inner upheaval was to finally bring me to the truths as I had never seen them before. I would struggle for another two years.

In the meantime, I was given the task of painting a cross on the small stoles which were placed in pixes, the small, gilded boxes which priests use to carry the Holy Eucharist to sick and dying persons. These pixes were sold in various bookstores owned and operated by the nuns. I was given very old oil paints and one old brush. When I protested that the oil was seeping into the purple fabric used to make the stoles, I was told to simply keep quiet and do my work. So, I made templates for three different style crosses. I hoped that, by so doing, the oil circle around the painted crosses would be diminished. I painted at least fifty of these stoles. This task was done in the sewing room where there were usually three or more other nuns present who were doing their personal mending or

Throwaway Nun

Rosemary Scirocco-Corsale
Kathleen A. Barreca

working on their sewing projects. I was usually silent during these recreation times except to ask for the necessary permissions. It was in the sewing room that I first heard the grumblings about the American Province and Mother Pietra directly from the lips of those nuns who were recent arrivals to the United States from Italy. At first, I was somewhat shocked. Even so, I never lifted my head from my work, and I never made a comment. Since I spent very little time in the sewing room, I was not always aware of the complaints by these nuns. However, I became aware of the bubbling teapot.

During the early months of the turmoil's and accusations that Sr. Jerald hurled against me during the retreats, I did what I always did—I retreated into my inner self, scolded and accused myself, and reprimanded myself over and over again. I would make resolutions to counter these terrible faults and bad examples. I would say extra prayers in reparation, and I would try to make additional mortifications and acts of self-abnegation to offer to the Lord and His Holy Mother, Mary, to seek help in eradicating these evil things from my character and behavior. There were long, soul-searching examinations of conscience, there were daily lists of actions in order to help recognize these serious problems, there were prayers cascading from droopy eyes wanting to fall asleep, but whose soul was too distraught for rest. I had been taught that my faults, failings, and defects would be pointed out to me by those who cared for me and wanted to see me become a saint. I never questioned Sr. Jerald, and I never doubted her accusations, that is, not during the first three or four months.

My vigilance in examining my conscience and making the lists produced nothing. The accusations and upbraiding did not hold up to the truth during these deep soul-searching periods. This caused me even

Throwaway Nun

Rosemary Scirocco-Corsale
Kathleen A. Barreca

further conflict and inner turmoil. I was convinced that I was being possessed by the devil, and that I was too evil to see my faults and failings. I trembled at each discovery which did not fit the accusations; I was questioning the authority and wisdom of mother superior, and, therefore, God, Himself! I was getting doubts about the accusation, and I feared that I would be cast far away from the mercies of the Lord Jesus. I was experiencing such inner conflict that my stomach would actually tighten, and there were many nights of little sleep. I did not discuss the state of my soul with anyone. I had learned that to trust anyone would be to risk further condemnation. I kept everything seething inside. On the exterior, no one could possibly tell what was going on. I worked hard, smiled a lot, and kept quiet.

The torment was so great that I thought I would lose my mind. Nothing Sr. Jerald accused me of made sense or proved real in my own watchfulness. With great intepridation, I had to put some of these things to the test. Mother Pietra was coming to Staten Island in June. From the time of her arrival until her departure three days later, I said exactly these words, "Praised be Jesus Christ," once in greeting Mother Pietra, once in bidding her farewell; and, "Yes," once in response to a senior nun's question. Lo and behold, as soon as Mother Pietra had departed, I was called aside by Sr. Jerald and severely scolded for monopolizing the conversation! I immediately went into the chapel and knelt on my knees. I did not understand what was going on; I did not understand why this was happening. I knew that I could do one of two things: I could accept the accusations and take responsibility for them, or I could opt for the truth. I chose the truth; the battle had begun!

Throwaway Nun

Rosemary Scirocco-Corsale
Kathleen A. Barreca

Over the next months, each and every accusation would be put to the test. The monopolization of conversations proved not true. Being a bad influence on others proved not to be true. Allowing me to be influenced by Sr. Mary of the Holy Innocents proved not to be true. I examined each occasion with great scrupulousness. Each accusation proved not to be true; but, this realization caused me no consolation and no comfort. I felt like I was betraying everything my religious life stood for! I felt like a traitor and a rebellious nun no longer worthy to be a bride of Christ. I ached to tell someone of the turmoil's and confusions of my soul, to unburden my state of mind, and relieve what I thought to be betrayal. But, I kept these things to myself. The trials of verification of the accusations occurred many times because I did not want to be deceived by my own doings. Each time, my soul plunged further and further into conflict. During quiet moments and even at prayer time, I began to get flashes of the past nine years. Although very upsetting, I could no longer stem the tide of these occurrences nor did I really want to. The many occasions of name-calling screamed into memory. I relived the emotions of hearing these names imposed upon me. Was I really stupid, ignorant, and retarded? If I were so backward, would I be so conscious of my surroundings and so sensitive to the conflicts of my mind and soul? Would I be so interested in reading, and could I learn new things so quickly? I was not stupid, I was not retarded! When I was a postulant in the motherhouse, I was told that the good Lord had endowed me with strength instead of brains and that I was to do hard, manual labor. I was still treated as an unintelligent person, and every day proved to be the exercise of the brawn and not the brain. I did as I was told in all instances. Through all the hard work, I developed

Throwaway Nun

**Rosemary Scirocco-Corsale
Kathleen A. Barreca**

masculine biceps. I was able to lift the wooden cases that weighed up to three hundred pounds or more.

Other occurrences also flashed into memory. I was often accused of being distracted and lacking generosity to the congregation. I discovered that I was not more distracted than any other human being and that my small errors were natural. I could not chastise myself for any lack of generosity. I examined my conscience again and again on this issue. I knew that I did more work than most others; I never hesitated to offer assistance to others, and I never shirked any work detail. I gave all of myself to my work. And so the flashes occurred with regularity; so did the intense scrutiny. I was beginning to be plagued by the "why" of it all. Why was I being treated in this way? Why was I so deprecated? Why was I not valued as a good, hardworking nun? Why was the amount and quality of my work never criticized? Why my internal life of prayer was never questioned? Why was I a scapegoat?

I began to be increasingly sensitive to what was happening around me. I began to watch the other nuns more closely. There were a few nuns who were very eager to be in the good graces of Mother Pietra. They would report every small thing to her. I soon learned that they would exaggerate the facts to make themselves look even better. As an example, early one morning while I was in the station wagon with other nuns on our way to sell books, one of the nuns asked another about her shoes. The second nun would take several pairs of shoes to a cobbler for repair. I also had a pair of shoes that needed fixed. I asked when our shoes would be finished, and I calmly added that the pair on my feet would soon have holes in the soles if I did not get the newly repaired ones back soon. Sr. Mary Anton, the driver of the station wagon and one of Mother Pietra's

Throwaway Nun

faithful informants, spoke up. She scolded me by saying that my comment showed my lack of generosity to the congregation and that I was ungrateful for all the shoes given to me by the superiors. I don't know what prompted me, but I responded, "From the beginning of my entrance into the convent, my parents had given me every pair of shoes and has had them repaired, as well." I stated that this was the first time that I had ever had a benefactor fix my shoes. Sr. Mary Anton angrily announced that she would report my "insolence" to Mother Pietra. I soon got my shoes back, and I never did hear anything more about my insolence, probably because Sr. Mary Anton was informed that what I had said was the truth. Close observation revealed that Sr. Adele *(my senior in Rhode Island during the incidences of the sputum in my soda pop, the long hair in our dessert, and my evening of emeses)* was a very passive, concrete person who could not handle anything out of the ordinary. Her passiveness was why she did not react, help, or comment when those unusual events happened in Rhode Island. She was one of the "reporters" to Mother Pietra, and glowed in every small recognition by her. Close observation revealed facts about Sr. Sara, the eldest of the nuns and to whom everyone turned for medical information and treatment. Sr. Sara knew much about home and old-world-farmers' remedies *(unfortunately, she was unable to do anything about her own arthritis)*. She is still living and well into her nineties as this book goes to press. Some of her remedies consisted of bitter drink used in Italy for fatigue and sluggishness. Any problems of the eyes were washed out with boric acid—that was to cure all eye ailments except the need for corrective lenses. Each fall, everyone lined up for a daily dose of cod liver oil which was to prevent colds, ague, flu, and sore throats. I was very susceptible to colds and laryngitis during the winter months. I was

Throwaway Nun

Rosemary Scirocco-Corsale
Kathleen A. Barreca

accused of not taking a full spoon of cod liver oil, not wrapping a thin shawl around me often enough, and of wanting to be sick. However, when I was ill, I never spent a day in bed nor remained at the convent when I was expected to work! Also, notice was now taken of Sr. Jerald, the superior, who not only fostered negative behavior, but was herself, one of Mother Pietra's faithful reporters and "worshippers." There were a few nuns who tried to get away with doing the least amount of work. They acted busy and were very good at disguising their ploys. They always welcomed a helping hand and often the majority of the job was left to the helper. As I reviewed this scene of convent inhabitants over and over, I discovered the key to my current woes! There were many nuns who grumbled and complained about the amount of work put upon them. They commented that they had never worked that hard in Italy. They were increasingly disgruntled over the autocratic and dictatorial manner with which Mother Pietra ran the American Province. They were unhappy about the "forced adulation" they had to render to her. These nuns did not hesitate to write to Rome to the Mother General about these matters. In fact, so loud was the complaining that Mother Pietra was called to Rome where she spent almost an entire year. However, she prevailed and became the chauffeur for the Mother General who took this opportunity to travel up and down Italy visiting each convent. But Mother Pietra returned from this trip ever more fervent in her mission to keep her status in the United States and to keep the adulation of the nuns. I became increasingly aware that whenever there were loud spurts of these complaints, so much more Sr. Jerald would criticize and scold me! So, I knew unequivocally that I was the scapegoat!

Throwaway Nun

Rosemary Scirocco-Corsale
Kathleen A. Barreca

When I really understood my scapegoat status my inner self was plunged into further turmoil. I examined and re-examined the last eight years. I continued to do the "testing." I hoped and prayed that my way would be illuminated by the Holy Spirit and that my findings would be wrong. At the same time I felt trapped. I did not want to leave the convent, but I did not have coping skills to deal with the situation.

In October, 1956, there was the first and only national exhibit of all religious orders in the United States. Each order of nuns was to set up an information booth in Philadelphia's Convention Hall. The booth was to hold pictures, memorabilia, and anything else that would identify the mission and purpose of the congregation. The exhibition was intended to showcase religious life, increase vocations, and to give Roman Catholics and non-Catholics alike the first comprehensive view of nuns. This exhibit was to last for four days. Sr. Mary Alice, who had been my Mistress of Postulants for two years and who had struck my face, was to spearhead the setup of our booth and the schedule of those who would tend to the booth from morning until ten o'clock at night. On the second day after the opening, I was sent to Philadelphia with Sr. Mary Adele to help out with the exhibit. In reality, I was sent to do all of the heavy work. After selling books and pamphlets all day long, Sr. Mary Adele would order a taxi to which I was to carry and load four to six heavy boxes of books. Each evening when we arrived at the back door of the convention hall, Sr. Mary Adele would stand near the boxes as I would carry two at a time to the booth. After the last of the boxes were unloaded, Sr. Mary Adele would stop by the booth not to be seen again until closing time at ten p.m. I would remain at the booth until both of the other nuns had gone to supper. When they returned, I would go to supper with the warning not to delay more than 45 minutes. After dinner on the third evening, I returned to the booth. The convention hall was overflowing with visitors. On the table in front of the booth was a stack of brochures explaining the mission and purpose of the Daughters of the Holy Word; the brochure was well done, that is, it was in full color, had various pictures, and presented nicely. Tucked inside of each brochure were a list of publications and an address list of other convents in the U.S.A. I noticed the crowds of people jostling to reach for the brochures. I instinctively picked up a handful of the brochures and began to distribute them to each person. I also began inviting the visitors to go into the booth to look at the large display of books and pamphlets nicely appointed on a table toward the back. I was somewhat surprised when I observed Sr. Mary Alice and the other nun selling the printed materials, since the rule of the hall prohibited any sales during the four-day exhibition. I extended the little invitation continuously for over two and one-half hours. When there was a lull in the crowds, I stopped talking and simply handed out the brochures with a smile and a "God bless you." Within ten minutes, Sr. Mary Alice turned toward me. At that precise moment, about twelve persons arrived in front of the booth. Sr. Mary Alice said, "Come on, send them in. What are you waiting for?" It was not what she said, but how she said it! The visitors froze in their spots and looked at Sr. Mary Alice and then at me. Her voice was degrading, reprimanding, and severe. I had not expected this upbraiding in public and before so many people! After a few seconds to regain my senses, I smiled, and talked on. By the end of the evening, I was developing laryngitis. This was another example of how little regard the nuns held for me, of the way they exploited me, and of the manner in which they assailed me. But, this had been the first time that such

Throwaway Nun

Rosemary Scirocco-Corsale
Kathleen A. Barreca

castigation had occurred in public. And, it would set in motion an entirely new arena of conflict and pain.

Sr. Mary Alice and the other nun, Sr. Jonathan, left to return to Boston. After doing the heavy work of tearing down the booth, Sr. Mary Adele and I departed for Staten Island. As usual, as soon as Sr. Jerald heard my raspy voice she scolded me for causing the laryngitis, and warned me not to make it develop into a bad upper respiratory infection. The end result was a few more days of sniffles; I was grateful that my voice returned soon.

About a week after returning to Staten Island from Philadelphia, I began having mild diarrhea. It did not impair my daily functioning; I completed all of my chores, and had no difficulty eating. The mildness of the problem caused me to not have to go to the bathroom often. This occurred at the end of October, 1956, and the month of November passed without my recollection of anything extraordinary. At the beginning of the second week of December, illness struck the convent. Of the twenty-one nuns there, nineteen contracted the flu. Only Sr. Jerald and I had been spared. Although my diarrhea was becoming worse, I dared not mention my own problems with so many nuns who were ill. Therefore, for the following ten days, Sr. Jerald cooked the three daily means, and I would carry the trays starting from the third floor to the second. We had no elevator, and I could only carry one tray at a time. When all of the trays had been distributed, Sr. Jerald and I would eat our meal. Then, I would collect all the trays and take them to the kitchen. After washing and drying all of the dishes and trays, I would help prepare for our next meal. The doctor was called and he came to examine each nun. He prescribed medications for each one; Sr. Jerald supervised the task of handing them

Throwaway Nun

**Rosemary Scirocco-Corsale
Kathleen A. Barreca**

out. A few of the nuns were well in three or four days, but the majority of them were in bed for more than a week. A retired registered nurse, Mrs. LaCivit, who lived near the convent, was often called upon to lend her expertise in caring for an ill nun. I asked Sr. Jerald if she would ask the nurse about the best treatment for diarrhea. Sr. Jerald said that Mrs. LaCivit had told her that I was to drink tea. So, each evening I was given a cup of tea, and each day the diarrhea got worse. I was bleeding rectally, enduring abdominal spasms, and feeling very tired. In the nine years of my religious life, I had never had any serious medical problems. The general assumption was that I was very strong and tireless. Hence, Sr. Jerald never asked what my medical problem was when I asked her to get the information from the nurse. Since the nuns had been bedridden with the flu for over a week before the Christmas holiday, Sr. Jerald urged everyone to do their best to make the time lost during their illnesses. The Christmas Holiday was, and remains, a very profitable time for religious, charitable organizations, and other projects. It is even more profitable if the donor is before the company of a nun; the donor is more likely to give more money. And so the rush was on to cover the areas which were most lucrative during the holidays. There was no time for me to be sick! Mail orders were sent out every day. The shelves had to be stocked every day. My chores had to be completed before breakfast each day because I had to be ready to leave with the other nuns to sell books and collect donated items. Yet, every day I was becoming more ill. When out with a senior nun, I tried very hard not to go to the bathroom; there were several nuns who took umbrage with my having to stop. This caused great spasms and pain in my abdomen. When I returned to the convent each evening, I would make the stop to the lavatory a priority. Most times, I had passed a

Throwaway Nun

Rosemary Scirocco-Corsale
Kathleen A. Barreca

lot of bright red blood. The pain was starting to last all during my waking hours. I started to pray each day that the day's end would come quickly. I fell asleep each night as soon as my head rested on the pillow. When the morning alarm rang at 5:30, I began to feel that I had barely slept an hour. I was sick and getting worse! Still, I told no one. After New Year's Day, 1957, Mother Pietra came to the convent for a few days visit. I asked Sr. Jerald to tell her that I was ill. After she had departed, I asked Sr. Jerald what she had said about my being ill. The response stung severely and felt as though it was being engraved on my forehead in fire! Mother Pietra had said, "Una suora con la faccia bianco e rossa non puo' essere ammalata." The translation is, "A sister with peaches and cream complexion cannot be sick." I knew not to protest or to make any further request for medical aid. I continued my daily routine with the myriad of chores. I endured the severe pain, never letting my face show anything but a "flat" look. To help myself, (*though now I know it was the wrong thing to do*) I ate every meal with two large slices of bread and I drank a small glass of wine hoping that my blood would be fortified or replaced. And, notwithstanding that I was becoming weaker and weaker, I prayed fervently for health. There was no reprieve from the abdominal pain. I could not ask for help because the superiors did not believe me, nor would they believe me. One morning, when I started my chores on the third floor, I was so bent over in pain that I laid down on my bed. Within minutes, Sr. Francine came into the room. She came over to my bed and asked what was wrong, but I did not have to answer....she saw that I was in trouble. She said that she was going to tell Sr. Jerald that I was very sick. I sat on the edge of the bed and begged her not to go to anyone because I would be severely reprimanded and publicly humiliated. Sr. Francine stared at me for several seconds; she

Throwaway Nun

**Rosemary Scirocco-Corsale
Kathleen A. Barreca**

understood because it had happened so often. She did not tell and I was very grateful. Over the next several days, I would catch Sr. Francine looking at me, but she kept my secret. Exactly on January 29, 1957, I went out selling books with Sr. Peter. We were in the business district of Newark, NJ. As the day wore on, I became chilled. My head seemed to be buzzing, my throat felt like it was constricting, and I could not get enough air. Each step was increasingly painful as each muscle screamed. In the afternoon, I told Sr. Peter that I was not feeling well. Kindly and patiently she said that we would go slower and take rests whenever we found chairs that we could sit on. She knew that if she were to take me back to the convent early, we would both be reprimanded. Besides, Mother Pietra was arriving that very day, and our returning between five and six p.m. would be very pleasing to her and Sr. Jerald; it would mean that we were out selling the entire day. That day seemed like it would never end. When we finally descended the stairs to the subway for our return to the convent, I was relieved. I felt so ill, I was not sure that I could get up the several flights of stairs before us and to the Staten Island ferryboat. Since it was winter, I knew that we would not be walking up the St. George hill to the convent, but that we would get a ride either with the convent station wagon or the bus. I was actually overjoyed when I saw Sr. Mary Anton on the ferry; she was driving the station wagon that day to collect donated items and she came looking for nuns who needed a ride home. When we arrived at the convent, Mother Pietra and Sr. Jerald were in the kitchen greeting the returning nuns and serving them espresso or cappuccino coffee as was the daily custom. I was relieved to be home and after greeting them, Mother Pietra pointed to me and said to Sr. Jerald, "This daughter is sick. After supper, we will send her to bed." This took me aback since I had no idea that my face showed how truly ill I felt. But I was glad that I would go to bed early; I felt that I could easily fall down from exhaustion and pain. Supper was usually served about seven o'clock in the evening. Our after-meal prayers were said between 7:45 and 8 p.m. However, it would be almost 8:30 that evening because Mother Pietra would share with us about new books and pamphlets at press, news from Rome, and exhortations. When I was finished bringing my plates and silverware into the kitchen for washing, I was called by Sr. Jerald. She informed me that I was needed in the garage to steel strap the cases ready for shipment. She told me to follow her. As soon as we exited the door, I gently reminded Sr. Jerald that I was not feeling well. In no uncertain terms, she told me that I would go to bed and rest after my work in the garage was done. Each of the cases weighed 300 pounds or more. I was to lift each one on a steel pipe and roll the case to strap it on both ends and in the middle. The memory of that night in the garage doing that very heavy work still causes me "physical pain." It was 12:30 a.m. when I finished my work and Sr. Jerald told me to go to bed. The other nuns had said community night prayers and had been in bed since 9:30 p.m. I only remember my sheer exhaustion. In the morning as I dressed, I realized that I simply was so tired that I could barely walk or use my extremities. I did not comb and braid my hair that morning; I merely combed it back into a bun as best I could. I descended the stairs and went into the chapel where we completed our morning prayers. The priest was ready to begin daily mass. The celebrant was Father Vincent. I was seated in the first seat in the first pew to the left of the altar. I was in the pew alone, but this was a common occurrence. I was kneeling and following the liturgy with my prayer book (which I still have) when Father Vincent had begun the

Throwaway Nun

**Rosemary Scirocco-Corsale
Kathleen A. Barreca**

Consecration, that is, the turning of the bread and wine into the Body and Blood of Jesus. I vividly recall that blackness enveloped me! When I awoke, I was on the floor and the back pew had been pushed away to give me space. I was unconscious for some time because when I regained consciousness, Mass was near the end. When I tried to get up, Mother Pietra was at my side helping me. She escorted me out of the chapel and brought me to the sewing room. She told me to lie down on a cot until everyone had exited the chapel. I was not sure exactly what had happened to me. Slowly, I realized that I had fainted. I was so sick that I did not panic that I would get a scolding from Sr. Jerald or Mother Pietra. Sr. Jerald came to me and told me to go upstairs, undress, and lie on one of the beds in the infirmary. My breakfast was brought to me by one of the nuns. Sr. Jerald brought me lunch and came to take the tray away. All day, neither she nor Mother Pietra asked me how I felt, gave me no water or other beverage to drink except at mealtime, nor called Mrs. LaCivit for advice. In the late afternoon, I began to worry about what was going to happen. I recall using the bathroom many times; each time I passed the usual bright red blood. The spasms and pain were ever present. The fatigue was unrelenting. In addition, when the diarrhea began, the rash behind my ears had resurfaced and it was bothersome and itchy. I had been able to request and receive a jar of petroleum jelly which I used to stem the terrible itchiness and retard the development of scabs. I prayed whenever I was awake. In the late evening, I heard the familiar doorbell ringing of the nuns returning from their rounds throughout the New York City area. At suppertime, Sr. Jerald came to the second-floor infirmary with my tray of food. She left and returned a minute later with the special white "underclothing" that was reserved for anyone having to see a doctor.

Throwaway Nun   Rosemary Scirocco-Corsale
                    Kathleen A. Barreca

She instructed me to put them on after I finished my meal. Though Sr. Jerald did not say anything, I knew that I was going to see a doctor. After the nuns had their supper, Sr. Jerald came to tell me to get dressed. When I had finished, I stood near the bed waiting for the next order. She came into the room and told me that she was taking me to see Doctor Timpi, the physician for the nuns. At 7:30 p.m. when we left for the appointment; it was already nighttime. I wrapped my light shawl about me to ward off the cold. Sr. Jerald did not speak one word going to or returning from the appointment; neither did I. I had long learned to keep silent. When it was my turn to see the doctor, Sr. Jerald explained that I had passed out. The doctor turned to me and asked what I thought the problem might be. I told him about the diarrhea, the abdominal spasms, the pain and the duration of these symptoms....soon to be four months. Sr. Jerald simply listened and said nothing. I was taken to the examination room, told to remove all of my clothing, and to wear the white gown with the opening in the back. Sr. Jerald was in the room and turned her back while I undressed. She never left the room, not even during my proctologic examination. All I heard was the doctor saying, "Oh, my God," with each twist of the speculum which is used for such an exam. He said that three times. I recall the pain of the exam, and how I nearly passed out again when the doctor requested a change of position. I was relieved when the examination was finished. Both Sr. Jerald and I went into Dr. Timpi's private office. After he sat down at his desk he said, "You are very sick, Sister. You have bleeding ulcerative colitis. I want you on bed rest for one month, no working, no worries." He then proceeded to prescribe a number of medications including intramuscular injections of cortisone, imferon, and Vitamin B12. Other medications were sulfa and a narcotic to ease the peristaltic action

Throwaway Nun

Rosemary Scirocco-Corsale
Kathleen A. Barreca

of the bowel. Dr. Timpi turned to Sr. Jerald and told her that I was to begin a strict bland diet; I was to avoid all fried foods, highly seasoned food, and anything containing acids. I was somewhat dismayed at all the medications I was required to take and the special diet he required. Since I had never been ill before, the idea of illness intimidated me. When we returned to the convent, the other nuns had finished night prayers and were going upstairs to sleep. I recall that sight as though it occurred just yesterday. Mother Pietra met us at the door. Sr. Jerald's facial expression was very somber, and I saw Mother Pietra show a look of concern as she glanced at me. She told me to go to bed and to say my prayers in bed. Sr. Jerald reported to Mother Pietra; I was never asked any questions nor permitted to be present at this report.

The next morning, Sr. Jerald came to the third-floor bedroom and told me to stay in bed. As she said this, the 5:30 a.m. bell rang. Sr. Monica was the only other nun sharing this three-bed room. The third bed was empty. When all was quiet, I began praying and fell asleep. I was aroused by a nun bringing me a breakfast tray. It consisted of a soft-cooked egg, two slices of toast, and a cup of coffee. After I had eaten, I got up out of bed and placed the tray on the bureau near the door. I heard the convent get very quiet; I knew the nuns had departed to sell books and get donations. I knew that Mother Pietra and Sr. Jerald were the only ones at home. I shuttered to think that I might be severely reprimanded by them both for my illness. However, this was not the case. Sr. Jerald came into my room to tell me that I was to move into the infirmary. I dressed and went to the second floor. I slipped quietly into the first bed. I could hear Mother Pietra shuffling some papers and answering the telephone in her office which was on the second floor and close to the infirmary. However,

Throwaway Nun

Rosemary Scirocco-Corsale
Kathleen A. Barreca

she never came into the room. At lunchtime, I was given several oral medications to take with a small glass of juice. Later in the afternoon, Mrs. LaCivit came to give me my three injections. I stayed in the infirmary for more than two weeks. Mother Pietra had left Staten Island and I never saw her. Neither did I see any of the other nuns. None came to the infirmary, and I did not ask to see anyone. Breakfast and dinner were always brought by different nuns who merely nodded their heads and said nothing. My breakfast was previously described. Lunch was a bowl of chicken soup with variations of rice or small pasta, bread and milk. Dinner was more elaborate with chicken soup, boiled vegetables, baked meat, and an occasional baked potato. I knew that my food was being prepared especially for me. But soon, this would change!

During the entire month that I spent in bed, Sr. Jerald came to the infirmary a few times to either bring a meal tray or take one away. At no time was I ever talked to, asked how I was feeling. I was left alone. The future was never discussed, and I did not ask. In retrospect, I often wondered why Dr. Timpi never hospitalized me if he thought that I was so ill. During this time, Sr. Jerald was pleasant and I was not hassled in any way. Only Mrs. LaCivit would come to give me my injections, and she was always cheery and kind. However, I dared not show any appreciation for her visits lest there would be reprisals.

I scarcely recall what state of mind I was in during this month. I remember being very relieved at the lack of almost daily upbraiding and scolding's. I rested a good deal of the time, and I recall praying a lot. I prayed for my health and for restoration of energy and strength.

When the month was over, I was well-rested, had more energy, and felt much stronger than I had in months. But I still had diarrhea, though it

Throwaway Nun

Rosemary Scirocco-Corsale
Kathleen A. Barreca

greatly abated and I was no longer experiencing the terrible spasms and pains. I was now out of bed and permitted to attend daily mass and prayers in the chapel, take meals with the community, and mingle during the hour of recreation in the evening. No one ever asked me anything about my condition and I never volunteered information. I knew that to do so would be to incur the wrath of my superiors. After the noon meal, I was sent to my own room for an hour nap. Sr. Jerald was always home and, after a few days, she told me that I could go to the cellar to do some "light" work. This involved doing the mailing, stacking the shelves, and sweeping. When I descended, it was apparent that no one had taken over my chores except for shelving the books and pamphlets. So I busied myself with sweeping, removing garbage from the trash cans, straightening out the various stacks of pamphlets, restocking shelves, and washing off the table tops. I no longer did all the chores in the mornings before breakfast; they had been assigned to others. Within days of tolerating my work in the cellar, I was washing the breakfast dishes and putting them away, and setting the refectory tables for dinner. All this time, I wondered just when the boom would be lowered; I didn't have to wait long.

After the second week of my being up and tolerating my chores, Sr. Jerald asked if all my symptoms had now been resolved. When I answered honestly that they had not but that they had abated, she proceeded to say things I still feel burning in my ears! In her usual, harsh voice, she said that I was deliberately "staying sick" and that I had been given enough time to rest and recuperate. The coup de grace came when she solemnly told me that I was young and needed medicine which was costing the congregation a lot of money, and that I was becoming a burden to the order! I felt my head pound, my abdomen tighten, and my stomach

Throwaway Nun

Rosemary Scirocco-Corsale
Kathleen A. Barreca

do a flip. Whatever respite I had been given during the past six weeks was over! The next day, my diet was changed. Breakfast remained the same. However, for lunch and dinner I was to eat a large bowl of rice cooked in milk, raw liver cut in cubes, creamed spinach, and bread. My diet would only change on Sundays when I was permitted to eat baked chicken and chicken soup for dinner. From the middle of March, 1957, until I left in 1958, my diet never changed! After three weeks, Sr. Marion bitterly complained one evening at the supper meal that she could no longer eat watching me eat the mound of raw liver! Others also assented, and from that day forward, I was to prepare my own meals with liver. I was to cut the liver in cubes and cook it in a frying pan until the burgundy color was gone. I was forbidden from actually cooking the liver, only to change its color to gray. It was still raw and difficult to chew and swallow. The others had stopped complaining and did not object to the deathly gray color. Even to this day, I do not eat rice and milk, creamed spinach, or any kind of liver. The idea of this kind of diet was that liver was best for making blood in the body and resolving anemia. But, it never helped.

    Mrs. LaCivit came in the evenings to give me my injections. One evening in the fall, Sr. Sara was in the parlor with Mrs. LaCivit and me. Mrs. LaCivit mentioned her concern for giving me the daily high doses of cortisone. She said that she had talked over the matter with a doctor friend of hers and he asked if I was still alive! That day was the last that Mrs. LaCivit came to give me my injections. The unpleasant task fell upon Sr. Florence. I continued to take all of the medications daily; I boiled the syringes for my injections. I ate my unpalatable diet of milk and rice, gray liver, and creamed spinach every evening, and I continued to be ill. The colitis would not abate. My stomach acted as though it was a circus act.

Throwaway Nun

**Rosemary Scirocco-Corsale
Kathleen A. Barreca**

Once, I asked to leave the dinner table and I went to the cellar bathroom to vomit. I felt terrible. When I came upstairs, everyone had already finished and the dishes were being washed. I reported to Sr. Jerald what had just happened and she coldly ordered me back to the refectory to finish my dinner. It took me a long time to finish. Remembering that event, I can still feel how each mouthful felt like a lump in my mouth and the actual pain of trying to swallow it.

My daily diet was a far cry from what the doctor ordered. But then I never saw Dr. Timpi after that first time. Nor was I sent to any specialist. So the pharmacy continued giving the multiple medications to the very end.

When I had been discovered ill, the scolding's, humiliations, and confrontations about my talking too much, being a bad example (but never telling me how and with whom), and exaggerating my small failures (like not being timely with setting out new materials to sell or not getting the ashes from the furnace to the curb in time), stopped; Sr. Jerald now concentrated on my illnesses. And the more she did so the more the colitis flared up, the more frequent the diarrhea, and the more spastic my stomach became. I was often told that I was keeping myself sick, that I had no desire to get well, that I was a real burden to the Order and costing them too much money for medications. I was told, in no uncertain terms over and over again, that my prayers and practices of piety were neither sincere nor strong because, if they were, I would then be cured! The more these accusations continued, the sicker I became. I had learned never to complain nor to tell anyone I was not feeling well. I knew I would never be believed. In addition, my mind had never stopped the barrage of

Throwaway Nun

Rosemary Scirocco-Corsale
Kathleen A. Barreca

awakenings about myself and the nine years that I had spent in the convent so far. Now, a new area of torment would besiege my mind and soul.

The more the days went by, the more I drew within myself. I had had periods of depression in the past, but I had always managed *(how, I don't know)* to crawl out of the hole. I was aware now that I was so depressed that I could not get on my feet. The black tunnel had enveloped me and there was no light at the end. I fought valiantly. I could not talk with anyone because I knew I would only incur more derision and problems. But, my mind would not quit; what I had discovered and was discovering about myself and this congregation tore through my body and soul like a double-edged sword. Not one day passed without the sword wreaking havoc on me; not one day did I experience a ray of joy, not one day did I enjoy peace of mind! What had I done to deserve this! What had I done that was bad, evil, or against the rules of this congregation? Why had I been so singularly abused?

No one noticed how quiet and introverted I had become over the last three years. As my illness continued and the depression engulfed me, my mind became like a never-ending motion picture. My life in the convent for the past nine years had brought me too many conclusions. I was definitely a scapegoat. Both the superiors and several of the senior nuns continued to be spies and reporters to Mother Pietra. Their fidelity to her every wish and whim was evident to me. Their caustic remarks to me and the wry smiles on their faces when I was publicly humiliated was clear evidence that I was their scapegoat. I was already aware that several of the nuns were unhappy about the way the order was run by Mother Pietra. I was aware that they wrote to Rome of their complaints and concerns often. I had already pieced together that when Sr. Jerald and/or

Throwaway Nun

**Rosemary Scirocco-Corsale
Kathleen A. Barreca**

Mother Pietra grew frustrated with them, I got unjustified and unmerited scolding. One day when I was in the kitchen washing dishes, Sr. Jerald began to reprimand me with accusations of sexual impropriety, disobedience, and violation of my religious vows. As she scolded, she walked in and out of the kitchen. The other nuns were departing for the day to sell books. They were all within earshot of this verbal tirade. I was dismayed; I knew nothing of what Sr. Jerald was saying. I did not understand her accusations. I was deeply disturbed. As usual, my abdomen tightened with spasms and pain, my stomach was in knots, and I thought I would not be able to keep down my breakfast. All of the nuns left and I was alone with Sr. Jerald. After completing the clean-up in the kitchen, I went to the cellar to do my chores. During lunch, Sr. Jerald was not unkind although very little was said. I searched her face for some explanation of why I had been so falsely accused that morning. She said nothing. All day, I examined my own conscience and could find not even an iota of wrongdoing. At 5 p.m., before the nuns began returning from their rounds, Sr. Jerald called me into the furnace room. There she perfunctorily told me that the accusations made against me in the morning were meant for another nun. "However," she said, "we can holler at you, but we can't say these things to the others." Her words stung. So now I had also become the "dumping ground" for the other nuns' degrations as well. When the community had gathered for dinner, Sr. Jerald made no attempts to clear me before the others. The next day, one of the nuns was taken to the airport and sent back to Italy. It seems that she had been trying to develop some liaison with a young, Italian priest. Though everyone knew about the abrupt departure and saw her, valise in hand, getting into the station wagon, there was not a word said to me. This happened rather

Throwaway Nun

Rosemary Scirocco-Corsale
Kathleen A. Barreca

often in the two years of my being in New York after my profession of vows. I had no mental tools to stem this tide. I simply screamed inside.

All my experiences with this congregation played themselves over and over in my head; the discoveries tortured my soul. I wondered why they referred to the Irish section of the Bronx in New York City as "giacometti" meaning drunkards. Yet, each Saturday, several pairs of nuns went to that neighborhood to sell books. I saw no drunks. What I did see was great respect for us everywhere we went. The people were very generous and kind. In several taverns, they had jars with the name of our Order on them. The senior nun would empty the jars after patrons had dropped change into them. I never witnessed anyone looking like those I saw lying in the streets in the Bowery section of Manhattan. What sort of prejudice was this? What stereotyped characterizations were cascading from the lips of nuns who professed kind words and Christ-like thoughts about all humanity? There were unkind words spoken about African American people, as well.

Once Sr. Mary Anton and I were knocking on doors in the Metropolitan Housing Development in the lower east side of New York City, where all of the occupants were of African- American descent. We knocked on a door and an obese, disheveled woman answered. Before I could say a word, Sr. Mary Anton said to me in Italian, "Che bel pezzo di cioccolato" meaning "What a piece of chocolate!" The comment was so unexpected that I stifled a laugh. The lady knew that she had been insulted calmly closed the door. Visits to depressed areas and to public housing were very rare because there was no money to be made there. The mission of bringing the Word of God to everyone, which was the real mission of the Order, was bypassed in favor of financial gain. Why, I wondered, was

Throwaway Nun

Rosemary Scirocco-Corsale
Kathleen A. Barreca

there a deliberate effort to avoid the poor and the needy? Where were the principles of nuns, the sight of whom was supposed to be spiritually provoking and good for the soul? Did not the African Americans and poor people need God's word and glad tidings? Why did the nuns harbor so much prejudice? Was this proper for nuns? When posted signs in many stores and factories read "No Solicitors," we had been instructed that these were never directed at us, and we were to disregard them. I never understood how the nuns could show such disrespect to these proprietors. Some places had dangerous machinery and equipment, and the signs prohibiting admission by visitors were posted with good reason. Very often, we would be escorted off the premises. The senior nun never missed making a comment after being sent away; it was never a prayer! We were grilled into not engaging with any one on religious topics nor to dally with anyone. The stock answer we were to give was, "We will pray for you. God Bless you." I recall the wailing of tears and sobs of a young girl whose fiancée had called off the wedding one week before the date. We knocked at her parents' door the day before the wedding. The senior nun said very little and extricated us from that apartment with the standard reply. Nothing was said to give the young girl hope for her future or even acknowledge her broken heart. There were many such incidents, some of which follow: A man with painful shingles, a recent widow, a cancer patient, hundreds of factory owners whose sewing machines were silent because their businesses were undergoing bad times. There were the very poor, and those searching for food in trash bins. On subways, there were very old and handicapped people, and pregnant women. On more than one occasion, I gave up my seat. The men in the greater New York City area notoriously do not give up their seats to those in need. I never saw a senior

Throwaway Nun

nun relegate her seat to anyone in need—not once! What were these nuns all about? I saw no true examples of Christian charity, no Christ like behaviors!

My "motion-picture" mind gave me no rest. Many things were very difficult to examine and seek the truth about in the miasma of deceit. There was any number of scams. Sadly, I recalled my own participation in many of them. The memory of those experiences caused me much grief. Elsewhere among these pages I talked about cases shipped to Italy that contained contraband among the things listed on the bills of laden. Also noted was the "handling" of the raffles held by the nuns. There were other scams. The few nuns who looked like they were in their late teens and early twenties were taken to benefactors to solicit a $50 donation which was to cover the cost of their habits *($50 was a lot of money in those days)*. The benefactors were told that the young nun had no parents and entered the congregation with no dowry. We were instructed to speak only Italian. Naturally, all of the benefactors were Italian. The same young nun was taken to several different benefactors. I was involved in three such scams.

When the scam was successful, everyone congratulated the participants. I grew appalled that I was made to participate in these unconscionable scams. There was another scam which involved the U. S. Customs Service. Mother Pietra was particularly pleased when boxes of religious articles would pass through customs without inspection. These articles were to be sold in stores throughout the United States; therefore, a duty or charge should have been paid. The customs officers could not have imagined in their wildest dreams that they were being duped by a religious order! Often, the nuns would show their unspecified appreciation by

Throwaway Nun

**Rosemary Scirocco-Corsale
Kathleen A. Barreca**

giving the officer a pair of rosary beads in a small leather case or some other small religious item. Time and time again, this would occur. Often, an airplane ticket or a passenger ship fare would be purchased for the sole purpose of shipping boxes of these religious items destined for market. I recall the nuns having difficulty with customs only a couple of times. This reeked of deception and the subverting of the customs laws of the United States! Again and again, Mother Pietra infused into the minds and attitudes of the nuns that we were above the law. What deceit in the name of Jesus! We were encouraged to "lie" about situations in order to get donations of specific items. For example, we would tell a pharmacist that several of the nuns were in bed with the flu and that we needed a donation of cough syrup or other flu preparations. Much of those donations were shipped to Italy in the case of used items. Whatever the Mother General told Mother Pietra was needed at the convents in Italy, she would order us to ask for these items as donations. When Rome finally built their large infirmary, pharmaceutical companies in the New York City area were approached for donations of medications which were shipped to Italy. The companies were told that we had an appropriately trained medical staff to dispense these medications. They never grew the wiser because these donors (like the customs officers) would never suspect that these pious-looking, gentle-speaking nuns could be so cunning. I grew to know that the scams and the deceit were elevated to an art!

There were so many such experiences, occasions of deception, and stretching of the truth that my head reeled and my soul ached. I was literally tortured. All this time, I never shared any of my thoughts with anyone. I never committed anything to writing because of my past experiences. What was left for me to conclude was that my entire

Throwaway Nun

Rosemary Scirocco-Corsale
Kathleen A. Barreca

existence took place in a den of phoniness, lies, and deception. I trembled, and I prayed more fervently than I had ever prayed in my life. I had been in the convent since I was thirteen years old. I knew that I did not have the know-how to extricate myself from these sad states of affairs. I did not have the verbal prowess to respond to the accusations, confrontations, and scolding leveled at me. Slowly I realized that my silence in all matters only increased the superiors' attitude that I was a simpleton with no brain. I felt trapped! I felt trapped with no way out! I did not want to leave the convent. I loved religious life, but not like I was living. To help stem the tide of these soul-wrenching thoughts occupying most of my quiet days, I asked if I could go out again to sell books and get donations. Sr. Jerald was only too willing to oblige; I was glad. So in April, I was out again six days a week. I must admit, that some care was taken not to send me with those senior nuns who would be carrying back bags of donated items. More than once, I was sent with Sr. Mary Anton who would be driving the station wagon; I would be able to avoid a full day of walking and climbing steps. It seemed that when I was out during the day, my abdomen and stomach were more relaxed. When I came back to the convent, I could feel myself tighten up again. I could feel gloom, I felt dark and more depressed!

In June, 1957, I was sent to the Motherhouse for a week-long retreat. I was glad to be away from New York City. I was delighted that I would be in silence and solitude for a week. During the past couple of years, I had become a very internal, introspective person and was very often alone with myself though many people might be around me. At the Motherhouse, I was happy to find that all but one of my co-novices was there for the retreat. I had not seen them in two years!

Throwaway Nun

Rosemary Scirocco-Corsale
Kathleen A. Barreca

The day after the retreat ended, five of us sat on the loading dock of the printer and talked until we heard the bell for night prayers. I did very little talking and no one seemed to take notice.

What I was hearing was very enlightening. Most talked about their disgruntled feelings and emotions, their disappointments in not achieving personal satisfaction in religious life, the emotions of anger and resentment they felt toward the superiors, and the ever-looming lack of the true spirit of the congregation. I was in disbelief because I thought that I was the only one who felt the negativity toward so many of the issues they spoke of that night! However, I never let them know of my assent; I never let them know of my feelings; I never let them know of my serious problems. I only knew that the situation of grumbling nuns was worse than I originally thought!

At first, I had gotten the impression that the dissatisfaction, grumblings, and rebellions came from the nuns who had immigrated from Italy and a couple of other foreign countries. Now, I became aware that the problems were universal! That night, I actually had difficulty falling asleep. I wondered how much more would be dumped on me; I wondered how far Mother Pietra and her cohorts would abuse me, it did not take long to find out!

That June, I stayed at the Motherhouse for a few days longer than ordinarily permitted; my parents had taken a train to visit me there. Because I was always so far away and air travel was not as popular as it is today, I received few visits from my family. So, this was an occasion and a real treat! As usual, my parents brought salami, ham, and boxes of canned goods to the convent. For two days, my parents ate their lunch and dinner in the visiting room at the Motherhouse together with a few other

Throwaway Nun

Rosemary Scirocco-Corsale
Kathleen A. Barreca

families who were visiting from out of town. In the past, I had been permitted to take all my meals with my visitors, and my parents were baffled and disappointed that I was not permitted to do so now. Also, I was never left alone with them! When I would join them after my meal in the refectory, I would go to the visitors' room accompanied by a senior nun who had specific instructions from Mother Pietra. So, my parents and I talked banalities, about each family member, and about each of them. I was forbidden to say anything about my health problems or about my diet. Since my diet had followed me to the Motherhouse, my parents would have been horrified to see me eating raw liver twice a day; hence, the denial of my taking meals with them. However, my mother noticed the rash that I had from mid-neck to my ear. When she asked what it was, the senior sister looked at me with a glance that I completely understood—I was not to tell them anything which would alert them or cause them concern. Always obedient, I brushed off the matter as being a small rash for which I was medicating (*I never told them that all I was permitted to use was petroleum jelly*). Assured that all was well, my parents left for Ohio the following morning and I quickly returned to Staten Island that very afternoon. Within a month, I was sent to see a dermatologist, Dr. Chiaramonte. When he examined my ears and the growing inflammation, he said that he was going to prescribe valium (*a medication to induce calmness*) because I had a serious nervous problem. So, valium was added to the list of daily medications, but it never helped cure the rash. The doctor did not prescribe any salve or ointment for the rash. I never saw the dermatologist again. I knew that the only reason I went this time was because my parents had not only noticed but had spoken their concern. Shortly thereafter, I went out with Sr. Mary Anton, a senior nun, to

Throwaway Nun

**Rosemary Scirocco-Corsale
Kathleen A. Barreca**

various places to pick up donations. While driving to Brooklyn, she asked what the dermatologist had said about my ears. I told her that Dr. Chiaramonte had diagnosed the problem as "nerves." She glanced quickly at me then proceeded to tell me that Mother Pietra did not believe in anyone having any form of nervous problems. I can still recall the dead silence that ensued and the words I used to break the silence; I said, "That's what the doctor said." I spoke very calmly and looked straight ahead at the road. Sr. Mary Anton glanced at me again and never commented. The very fact that I would respond seemed to surprise her. The matter of my illnesses was never mentioned again.

The conferences at each monthly retreat with Sr. Jerald were reprimands and scoldings regarding my health. In September, 1957, this conference would prove to be a turning point for me and my vocation! In her usual cold, mean voice, she told me that if I did not get better, I would be sent home. She proceeded to tell me that the congregation could not retain sick people that cost money and were unable to work as they should. She talked about the inconvenience of my special diet, my need for daily injections, the monthly cost of the medications, and my continuous ill health. Her words burned like fire in my soul as she pontificated, "Your body is sick because your soul is sick." I still don't know how I stayed seated in my chair! My head was reeling, my body was in contortions on the inside, and I felt like I would lose consciousness; but I did not. I had managed to keep my stone face throughout all this. After this confrontation, I went straight to the chapel. My body seemed to be on fire, and I knew not how to quell this outrage except to pray with all my might. There was no question that I was to be sent out of the convent and my religious vocation would be over—it was just a matter of time!

Throwaway Nun

**Rosemary Scirocco-Corsale
Kathleen A. Barreca**

For the next several weeks, my every thought was about my vocation and the gift of perseverance in religious life. I knew that I would not be given a chance to live the remainder of my life as a religious. I had been in the convent for ten years, and I feared facing the world outside! It was one that I had renounced and did not know. I thought about the extreme pain my leaving would cause my parents. I ruminated about their anger and disapproval. I did not know how they would react, so I worried. However, I later discovered that I did not have to spend these energies being concerned about my family's reaction to my departure from the convent. My parents, siblings, and their families would prove to be my strength, my support, and my source of encouragement. It was difficult for me to believe that they would actually send me out of the convent; in fact, the matter was incredible! I was a professed nun who had taken formal vows. I had been in the congregation for ten years. I had been as obedient as possible. On what grounds would they send me home? I understood why the young nun who tried to have a liaison with a young priest was sent back to Italy.

But, she remained a nun! I understood the reasons for sending home the novice and the postulant who were found in a sexually compromising position in the wee hours of the morning. I understood why Sr. Mary Peter was whisked away one afternoon in early 1957 after she was discovered to have been taking money from the bin of other senior nuns and placing it into her own cache of donations (she had done this to make it appear that the benefactors in her territory were more generous). She was sent back to Brazil, but remained in the convent! There were many other situations of nuns being out rightly rebellious, disobedient, and vocal. None of them were dismissed from the convent! I worked more

Throwaway Nun

**Rosemary Scirocco-Corsale
Kathleen A. Barreca**

than the others until I became ill! I had never violated my vows, had not been rebellious, nor vocalized any dissatisfaction! If I had, Sr. Jerald would never have taken me to the furnace room a few months earlier and told me that the senior nuns could holler and scold me because I could take it and never say a word, but they could not do so with the others. The scoldings, upbraidings, and humiliations were never about my spiritual state or the quantity or quality of my work. They were never about violations to the Constitution of the Congregation, or to the rule of obedience. Hence, how and on what grounds would they send me away? The Constitution was very clear about nuns who became ill; it dictated that the Order was to see to their medical needs and to obtain all of the services and medications necessary! It said nothing about sending a formally professed nun out of the convent for reasons of health! These thoughts began to occupy every waking hour, and I became more depressed. The colitis began to get worse; whatever small gain I had made in the past eight months were lost. I took the medications faithfully, but they no longer helped. It was during this time that I first prayed for death! I began to see death as the only way out of this mishmash of hypocrisy, deception, scape goating, and incurable illness. I found myself in a long, dark tunnel with no light at the end. I had no more reason to live; I felt trapped. I was trapped with no escape route in sight! For God to take me in death is what I prayed!

After the monthly retreat conference with Sr. Jerald, I penned a few of my thoughts and feelings confident that no one would ever see them. I was very sure never to allow my superiors to read my notes. On October 2, 195, I wrote:

Throwaway Nun

Rosemary Scirocco-Corsale
Kathleen A. Barreca

"It's so hard to face certain facts; this is once that I would really like to avoid the issue, but it's impossible. Why must I live with the dread and fear of the past and have it forever repeated. The same thing over and over: you'll be sent home! But, this time is the last; I'm just as fed up with it as my superiors. I don't want to live in fear the rest of my life. I want to love and live in love. I never thought I'd live through September 3, when Mother Pietra passed, me, but now I quit—I've given up myself completely to Jesus and Mary. There is nothing I can do with myself or for myself. I entrust my future, my being, my all to God's good pleasure; whatever He wants, how He wants, and when and where He wants. I ask for no graces except those that Jesus and Mary see I need the most according to their good pleasure. I am working hard to do it all— to abandon myself, wholly and without a fiber of reserve. It is so hard, but I must succeed with His grace because this is what God wants of me, I am sure. I must remember to say, 'By myself I can do nothing' as often as possible to excite sentiments diffident in myself and increase trust in abandonment in God. My health is so vital, so important, but I will not worry anymore.

Whatever God wants; I cry, I get nervous, I lose sleep worrying, but I leave it up to Jesus and Mary. Pray, have faith, and trust in God—abandon everything into His hands. Pray the rosary well. Pray, be recollected and God will provide. Don't let your imagination get the best. Put your life-body, soul, and future—into God's hands and forget about them. Trust in Our Lady. If God has permitted, for some better and far more perfect thing, for me to be so deeply engulfed in these great difficulties, I ask not that He takes it away and gives me consolation, but rather that He gives me grace and strength to live through it because I find

Throwaway Nun

**Rosemary Scirocco-Corsale
Kathleen A. Barreca**

myself at the bare end of human sustainment. Grant that I may love You, Lord, and do with me what You will."

In mid-October, 1957, I was privately told by Sr. Jerald that I was to take over the charge of the chapel. I was very surprised by this! Since that fateful day during my novitiate in 1954, I had never done any work or holiday preparations in the chapel. However, since I had been relieved of several heavy, laborious chores, it did not take long for me to understand why this task had been assigned to me. Cleaning, readying the altar for daily worship, changing the altar linens, arranging fresh flowers, and putting out new votive candles was not considered "hard work." In fact, the job had belonged to Sr. Mary Anton, one of Mother Pietra's favorite nuns. In addition, I had to set out the priest's vestments every day. I would do this task until the very end of my religious life.

What happened next was unexpected! Sr. Jerald told me that I was to practice playing the organ every Sunday during the recreation hour. I froze inside! The superiors knew that I had taken piano lessons when I was in grade school for about six to eight months. That occurred 16 years previously; I had not touched a musical instrument since. I fretted and worried. I was not told what was expected of me. So, I started practicing on the old, push-pedal organ which rested in the niche on the left of the first two pews. I remembered the scale, so I laboriously marked out the scale on a blank piece of paper. This is how I began learning to play "O, Salutaris" and 'Tantum Ergo," the two hymns which were sung during the Benediction of the Blessed Sacrament. By December, I had become very proficient in playing these two pieces of music, and I no longer had to rely on the paper upon which I wrote the scale. I had some difficulty with the positioning of my fingers because I could not remember the correct

Throwaway Nun

Rosemary Scirocco-Corsale
Kathleen A. Barreca

digitations. But, I forced myself to play the pieces easily. In December, as usual for every Christmas holiday, the organ was removed from the chapel and placed in the small pantry, which was within a few yards of the chapel entrance. There, I would practice on Sundays. One Sunday before Benediction, Sr. Jerald told me that I was to play the two pieces I had been practicing. All afternoon I trembled, but I knew that I could play these pieces flawlessly. At four p.m., the nuns gathered in the chapel. I sat at the organ, and I asked Sr. Teresita to remain at the entrance so that she could sing the first few bars in order to help the others to sing on key. When she refused, my stomach tightened. Needless to say, Sr. Lewis' voice bellowed and was not in tune with my playing. In my immaturity, I continued to play instead of just stopping. I do not know how it sounded in the chapel, but I was dismayed. I knew, unequivocally, that I had played the pieces correctly and in the proper tempo. After I finished playing, I waited in the kitchen for Mother Pietra and the others. When she confronted me, her face was reddened and her lips pursed; she was struggling hard not to berate me, as usual. She said that I played terribly and that I would never again play the organ. Sr. Teresita was right behind her. Our eyes met, and then she left the room. My blind obedience had once again blinded my intelligence! I had learned this lesson ten years earlier when I was told to read a book about art. My talent for art had been destroyed, my singing talents had been squelched, and now my bit of organ playing had been put to death. Outside of heavy labor and long hours of hard work, every talent I ever possessed had been somehow destroyed. I blamed myself for the organ fiasco until I later realized that Sr. Lewis had led the others to sing off key with her bellowing. I knew that I had done a phenomenal job of learning how to play the two hymns. Later, I would think that this was an

Throwaway Nun

**Rosemary Scirocco-Corsale
Kathleen A. Barreca**

effort by Mother Pietra to kill anything left in me with the usual excuse that I had been permitted to do everything that I wanted. So, 1958 did not have a very happy beginning for me; it would prove to be very painful and life-altering!

As the holidays approached, the convent buzzed with the flurry of activities for that time of year. I was still in charge of all of the mailings which I did every night. The senior nuns planned their daily route very carefully in order to get the largest monetary contributions and donations of items. Although there were crates being readied for shipment to Italy, I was no longer sent into the garage to steel-strap them. The Christmas holiday, which was and remains my favorite time of the year, was filled with depression and fear. Somehow, I knew that this would be my last Christmas in the convent. I went through my daily routines as though I were in a great fog. I now battled within myself every day—the struggle between wanting to die and wanting to stay in the convent. The battle was taking a greater toll than I anticipated!

In January, 1958, Mother Pietra made her usual start of the New Year visit. In retrospect, I knew that she came regularly at that time of year to oversee that the crates being shipped to Italy had enough good items like food and staples in them, and to be sure that they were hidden between the so-called used items. The most important reason she came to Staten Island was for the large amount of money they collected which she would send to Italy. The Daughters of the Holy Word Congregation in Rome was having a basilica built and most of the money for construction came from the United States. In addition, there were other constructions going on and Mother Pietra made sure that the financial needs were met. In the meantime, the convent in Staten Island, an old Victorian mansion,

Throwaway Nun

Rosemary Scirocco-Corsale
Kathleen A. Barreca

left much to be desired as a building. There was no such construction in the United States as there was in Italy. For this reason Mother Pietra was able to maintain her power and absolute authority in the American Province of the Order. She would never be deposed. However, the barrage of letters written to the Mother General in Rome with the myriads of complaints and concerns was ever increasing! This threatened the dictatorship of Mother Pietra, both directly and indirectly. In addition to the Italian nuns in America writing to Rome to complain, there was a host of American nuns doing the same thing. Mother Pietra was much disturbed about this situation.

One evening at the dinner table while Mother Pietra was still in Staten Island, I was to feel the lash of her tongue and gain a new insight. Without provocation and without justification, she announced to everyone that I was to be sent home! I was thunderstruck! I looked around and noticed everyone with their heads down on their plates. No one even dared look at me. At that moment, my whole body tensed and my insides twisted and turned. There was a deafening silence! Then, I heard a shrill, wailing cry come from the pit of my stomach. This sound struck me so much that I immediately looked around. To my amazement, everyone was still bent over their plates eating. Slowly, I realized that the scream had lodged in my throat and never escaped my lips. It would take over thirty years for that shrill scream to finally audibly erupt. Mother Pietra had chosen the right time and place to announce this. She deliberately wanted to capture the attention of the others, and, more importantly, to frighten them! She had succeeded beautifully! When no one broke the silence, she, herself, made a mundane statement to which several nuns picked up on; thus, the tension was broken. But I was left fatally wounded in combat. No one

Throwaway Nun

**Rosemary Scirocco-Corsale
Kathleen A. Barreca**

tended to my wounds, and I was again bleeding excessively. I continued to desire and pray for death, but this peace eluded me time and again.

I struggled each and every day. In addition to my bleeding ulcerative colitis and anemia, the diarrhea continued. With all my effort I learned to hold the urges to stop at restrooms while I was out daily selling books. When I arrived back at the convent each evening, the spastic pains were so severe that I asked permission to go to the bathroom before going to pray in the chapel. I would release, what appeared to me, much larger quantities of bright, red blood. I would fall asleep with the pain. I awoke the next morning free of spasms, at least for a little while. It was difficult combing my hair. The rash behind the ears was invading my scalp and large scabs covered my head. My thick, chestnut hair was no longer. It got very thin and scraggly. And, my stomach followed suit. I now lived with a spastic stomach and pain which did not end.

No one noticed my weight loss, my ashen face or a slowness in doing some chores and tasks which was unlike my past. And, I wrote the following:

February 3, 1958. My mind takes me through terror and torture at times, so much so that I have nightmares, I can't work or pray, or think of anything in those trances or fits. What is, will be. Have faith in Jesus and Mary. They'll always understand. Always there to spill the story to; always ready to hear and to show you that something is "not of this world." What of it, even if the superior doesn't like; Jesus and Mary count; nobody else. You live for them, nobody else. You struggle all this out for them. Give them honor as a token of gratitude for their mercy and graces. There are moments in which I cannot concentrate, can't think, except visualize terror in its worst. In those moments, I offer to the Lord, each moment as an act

Throwaway Nun

Rosemary Scirocco-Corsale
Kathleen A. Barreca

of love, and as a proof of my love for Him. In those dread moments, help me, Lord, think of You and I shall be consoled, uplifted and encouraged. Help me not to show anybody what I suffer inside—nobody. I don't ask to take the cross away, but for the strength to carry it. I don't think it's wrong not to tell the superior. You know I can't. It's impossible. I can't explain everything and it's unbelievable. But, I know You understand everything so well. Without any words, show me peace and rest from my mind.

February 6,1958. I was thrust for a few days in mental illness. I was upset, nervous and my mind wouldn't think of anything but terror of the future. Everything has faded away. God is so good! My trust is in Him. My hope, my love for Him, because I have, well learned that He is "He who is."

March 2, 1958. Health is vital for religious life. If I want health, I must pray, be good. Live well the religious life. "If you want help and the grace to give to you, live well your religious life, do well your duties. I always feel like a heel at every passing. If only I could put my desires, my heart, thoughts and my reflections into "life" I would sincerely be what the superiors want of me. It's in the actual doing that I fall short miles from the border. There is much to be desired. I am so distracted and so proud I only wish that my superiors could be pleased with me. It would mean so much to me. I have good will and good intentions. Make me live them daily. Grant me Your grace to live religious life well, to be what You have planned to make me. I need You so much in every day, every moment because of my misery and my nothingness. Help me, do not let my cry, Lord, rise to You in vain.

In the ensuing months, I knew I was growing weaker and weaker. I knew that Mother Pietra was waiting for an opportune time to send me

Throwaway Nun
Rosemary Scirocco-Corsale
Kathleen A. Barreca

home. She needed this drama to keep the other nuns in check and to try to diminish the myriads of letters Rome was receiving in no praise of her. During monthly retreats with Sr. Jerald, she would tell me that I was not praying enough, that I was losing my faith, and that I was too weak in piety. Did she think that I was possessed by some evil spirit? Mother Pietra, Sr. Jerald, and the other inner cohorts really believed that I made myself ill, that I could will myself to get better, and that I was deliberately keeping myself sick. Never did it occur to any of them that they might be the cause. Or, that the ten and a half years of ill-treatment and destruction of my self-worth, the constant badgering, the unfounded accusations, and the perpetual nagging just might be the reason for my illness. They never imagined that I caught on to the myriads of deceptions, briberies, lies, and unchristian like behaviors and attitudes, and that was what caused my inner self to rage with illness. They never did, and would not now, believe that they did or said anything improper. They could never admit their guilt or wrong-doing. I came to learn that men and women of the "cloth" feel that they are always right and that everyone else is wrong! To disagree with one or more of them is like challenging the Magisterium of the Roman Catholic Church. The Daughters of the Holy Word would defend themselves, even today, though it would mean fabrication and deceit. After all, who would doubt a nun? Sadly, I do!

In the interim, my mind would not be stilled, and I continued being tortured with revelations and truths to which I had been blind and to which I had come to believe in my blind obedience. Sr. Jerald noticed that I was getting weaker. Once or twice a week, I would be kept at home instead of going out to canvas. Since I had to ask the senior nun's permission to use the bathroom, they dutifully reported to Sr. Jerald that I would use the

Throwaway Nun

Rosemary Scirocco-Corsale
Kathleen A. Barreca

facility three or four times a day. At the same time, there was a marked decrease in my strength and energy level. My spirited, quick walk was reduced to one with effort. I was even having difficulty taking out the thumbtacks to replace the altar linens. I often asked for a hand from one of the nuns passing by. All of this was passed on to Sr. Jerald, as I later found out. They had reason to be concerned.

While all of these things were transpiring around me, I vowed that I would never ask to leave; I would force Mother Pietra and Sr. Jerald to cast me out of the Order! I would never believe that I did not have a religious vocation. I wanted them to have to face the Lord Jesus Who called me in the first place! I bargained with the Heavens, "I will never ask to leave, but if I am sent out, You will have to take care of me!" So, I reasoned that I would be faithful to my Spouse, Jesus, until our union would be killed by others and never by me. I wanted to be a nun all of my life. My dreams, my reality were being shattered. I knew that I had lived almost eleven years of hell; I had accepted it as my lot. Now, I was a throwaway nun!

The spring of 1958 was closing and summer would sprinkle sunshine everywhere. I was feeling poorly and my symptoms did not abate. My diet was the same, and I took my medications every day even though I had not seen a doctor for more than a year and a half. In my prayers, I begged of the Lord the strength to endure the pain and weakness; I begged for the favor of not fainting again. On three occasions, I can vividly recall my mind slipping. Once, I was sitting up in bed and I did not know what to do. I didn't know if I was supposed to go to sleep or to get up. When the other nun turned off the light, I laid my head on the pillow and went to sleep. It happened again at the dinner table. After

Throwaway Nun

Rosemary Scirocco-Corsale
Kathleen A. Barreca

saying the grace before my meal, I sat down and my mind went blank. It was only after looking at the nun across from me that I was jogged to the reality of having to eat my dinner. The worst of these memory lapses came one afternoon in late May. I was not sent out canvassing that day, but I had to do my chores in the cellar. When I reached the bottom of the stairs, I could not remember which way I was to go, what I had to do, or exactly why I was in the cellar. It seemed a long time before my memory returned and I proceeded with my tasks. More than once I would momentarily forget my name, and often, I was called twice before I responded. These gaps of memory bothered me because I wondered if others noticed my deficits.

As far as I could tell, no one noticed or ever commented. It would be a few years later that I would come to understand the danger and precariousness of these lapses of memory. I was very close to having a complete nervous breakdown! To this very day, I don't know nor understand why I did not lose my mind under the conditions of my life, or what spared me from this problem. All of the conditions were ripe, and certainly the traumatic stressors had wreaked enough havoc to have warranted a mental breakdown. Perhaps, after all, there was a faithful Guardian Angel sitting on my shoulder protecting me, but it was too dark for me to see the light!

Easter, 1958. "Pray—this is the hour of the greatest thing of your life; it's either in or out! Blessed Mother, I leave it all up to you. Guide me, protect me, and do with me according to God's Holy will. Show me His path and His Light, grant me His grace. Help me in this greatest hour of trial. Whatever it is, guide my soul to salvation."

Throwaway Nun

Rosemary Scirocco-Corsale
Kathleen A. Barreca

June 1, 1958. "All I ask is to do God's will, always, in all things, and that the hardest things are done to accomplish His will. So it occurred on the third day of July that I headed for home to stay out forever. The sensation, the feelings, the tears, the dread of night—I seem to have been in a dream. But now, on July 14, I am certain of vivid reality—lost dreams! I face the facts as God sends them, and I am certain that in the accomplishment of this arduous sacrifice that He showers His blessings not only on me, but on my beloved ones. For me, there exist no differences between life and death. I welcome death as liberation from this wicked world. I love to live only to help my fellow man. I put my life, my physical condition, and my all into the hands of our Blessed Mother that I do not mine, but Jesus' will always."

June 1, 1958. This is the end of the roads. I can't keep one foot here and one there; the break must come and I pray God it comes swiftly, that it be His will through all eternity. It is useless to put here in words the anguish, torture, and torments I have been subjected to for the past two years, but most atrociously during these past two months. My daily offering to Jesus and Mary of everything, both fears and tears, that the future would be a fulfillment of God's holy will. And my health plays odds against my vocations. My sickness is only because I have worried myself sick over my vocation. I am in such a mental and physical state now that I am very much confused, unsettled. Mother Jerald said I let myself fall so low, get so upset and worked up, and nervous. My failing health and increasing slowness did not escape the notice of the Superiors. One day in early June, I was told not to go out canvassing. After breakfast, Sr. Jerald told me to go upstairs in the infirmary where I would find the "whites," the underclothing used for doctor and hospital visits. I did what I was told. In

Throwaway Nun

**Rosemary Scirocco-Corsale
Kathleen A. Barreca**

mid-morning, Sr. Jerald told me that she would be taking me to a specialist in Long Island. I can't remember the doctor's name, but I recall that his office was directly across the street from St. Anthony's Hospital. Once in his office, I was not asked to undress. The doctor simply asked me several questions. More than once, Sr. Jerald answered for me. As I turned to leave, the doctor asked, "Sister, are you happy?" I was taken aback by this question. I shot a furtive look toward Sr. Jerald, and I saw her hands squeeze against each other. I simply said, "Yes." He looked at me intently; I thought he was able to read my mind! I quickly turned away from him to leave his office. Sr. Jerald followed. I waited near the door for her; she had remained behind and I could see her listening to the doctor and shaking her head. On the way back to the convent she said nothing, volunteered nothing, and looked straight ahead at the road. I did the same; I had learned my lessons well. Several days later, I was told to don the whites again. After the other nuns had left for the day, I was told that I would be admitted to St. Anthony's Hospital. I was told that the doctor had found me in a weakened condition and had informed Sr. Jerald that I needed blood transfusions.

I remember that day, it was June 13, St. Anthony of Padua's feast day. The sun was shining and there was the sweet smell of blossoms in the air. The drive to the hospital took almost one hour. Again, Sr. Jerald and I made a silent journey. I dared not show her that I was actually happy! I thought that this might be my final hour, and that I might die. I did not share any of my thoughts because I did not want to open up an avenue for her to mark me with her diatribes. I was too elated because I would soon die and go to heaven!

Throwaway Nun

Rosemary Scirocco-Corsale
Kathleen A. Barreca

When we arrived at the hospital, Sr. Jerald accompanied me to the admitting office. Then, she left. I was taken to a private room where the nurse asked me to remove my habit; I did not remove the "whites." I crawled into bed. I was so glad to be lying down; I was having a very difficult time standing and walking for even a short time. After the preliminaries, I was left alone and I soon fell asleep. I was awakened by the doctor's voice. He stood by the foot of the bed and said that I was to have blood transfusions which would be started immediately. I dozed off again and was awakened by a dietary aide who brought my dinner tray. When I took off the cover to my plate of food, I was pleasantly surprised. There on my plate was Salisbury steak, mashed potatoes and yellow squash. The single slice of bread was toasted and it came with a generous pat of butter. There was a carton of milk and a piece of unfrosted cake. I smiled, and actually ate heartily. After all, I had not had such delicious food in over a year and a half. For the duration of my hospital stay, I was served good-tasting food. I recalled how special the meals for Mother Pietra were after she had surgery a few years ago. Each dinner consisted of a fresh, grilled steak cooked by Sr. Jerald or Sr. Sara. She got either mashed or baked potatoes or another vegetable each day. They were sure that she did not get the same vegetable twice in a row. But then, I had not deserved anything better than my usual raw liver, creamed spinach, and rice cooked in milk. Good food was "intelligent" food; I was considered a "mammalucca" a stupid person or nerd. So without question, I enjoyed all of my meals while I was in the hospital. Needless to say, like the cola soda pop, I would never again eat liver, creamed spinach or rice in milk in my life.

Throwaway Nun

Rosemary Scirocco-Corsale
Kathleen A. Barreca

Each day, I was given a transfusion, and in the evening, a few vials of blood were taken. I was given several medications during the day. With the peaceful, quiet time, I prayed to the Lord freely and unabashedly. At the end of the third day, the doctor came into my room. He pulled the chair from the corner of the room and sat to my right near the foot of my bed. He looked somber. Slowly, he asked how I was doing and I answered as I usually did—that I was feeling fine. He nodded. What he said next has stayed with me in exactly the same words that he used. He said, "Today, I had a conference telephone call with Mother Pietra and Rome. It seems that your health has continued to fail in the convent. We talked about your going home to your parents until you can get better and stronger." He stopped and looked up at me. He had been staring at the floor until then. I looked back. He asked me if I understood what he was saying. I nodded affirmatively. I am sure that he was expecting some kind of outburst or even a muffled reaction. Instead, he saw the stone, expressionless fact that I had been so good at developing over the last years. He waited a minute more to see if I would exhibit any emotion in reaction to that sort of news. When there was none forthcoming, he got up and replaced the chair in the corner. He came back to my bedside and said that I would be discharged the next morning. I did not receive the results of the few tests taken or any follow-up instructions upon discharge.

The next morning, I asked permission from the nursing staff to get dressed so that I could go to the hospital chapel for morning liturgy. I went, and prayed heartily. After all, I had not died, and I had gotten the decision from the doctor about my future; I never saw the doctor again. The nursing staff had to call the convent to inform them of my discharge.

Throwaway Nun

Rosemary Scirocco-Corsale
Kathleen A. Barreca

In the three and one half days of my hospitalization, there had been neither visits nor any telephone calls to inquire about my health.

As I waited, I wondered why Mother Pietra had chosen to place the heavy burden of telling me about the conference call upon the doctor's shoulders. He was obviously very uncomfortable being the bearer of such horrible news. In reviewing these last days over and over in my mind, I concluded that Mother Pietra had no justifiable reason to send me out into the world and back to my parents. Having the conference call with the doctor and the Mother General in Rome, she could hide behind the problems of my health and have the approval of the doctor. In this manner, Rome would never fault her. At the same time, she could get away with her biggest plot to instill fear in the community, and thereby, decrease the overwhelming barrage of criticism of her activities to the Mother General in Rome! The other nuns were led to believe that my leaving was because I had been very disobedient and had become ill because of that disobedience. Only 20 years later would I know that Mother Pietra had called a meeting of all the nuns while I was sent for a Sunday afternoon nap. She asked the nuns what they thought about my being sent out of the convent. I was told that several nuns spoke in my defense saying that there was no good reason to take so drastic an action. I was also told that Mother Pietra's closets cohorts told her that whatever decisions she would make would get their approval. Too many others simply said nothing. Therefore, Mother Pietra had succeeded in her ulterior plan to leave the recalcitrant nuns in fear. If she had the power to send someone like me home, then they could also be cast out. If she could send me, who had no blemish other than severe illness, out, then they could also be cast out for their grumblings, criticisms, and deprecating letters to Rome.

Throwaway Nun

**Rosemary Scirocco-Corsale
Kathleen A. Barreca**

Notwithstanding this horrible sequence of events, I held on to the glimmer of hope—after all, I had not heard anything from Mother Pietra or Sr. Jerald about the conference call to Rome. It was time for the annual weeklong retreat. I was to renew my vows of chastity, poverty, and obedience for two more years. The yearly retreats were held at the Motherhouse; I was not sent! Instead, Mother Pietra came to Staten Island for another of her "visits." Since my return to the hospital, I was not permitted to leave the convent to go canvassing. Rather, I was instructed to take a nap in the morning and in the afternoons. One day, I was called to lunch. Mother Pietra, Sr. Jerald, and I were the only ones in the convent at that time. We had lunch in the kitchen; I sat to Mother Pietra's right. Sr. Jerald was directly across from me. When we had finished our soup; Mother Pietra began to talk to me. She averted my eyes as she usually did. She proceeded to tell me about the conference call between the doctor, herself, and the Mother General. My stomach tightened just a little. She repeated what the doctor had told me: that my remaining in the convent was detrimental to my health, and, therefore, I would be sent home. After she said this, she stopped talking and waited for me to react in some manner. However, I continued to eat my lunch. My nonchalance took them both by surprise as was shown on their faces. Mother Pietra proceeded to talk about my failing health, my not responding to various medications, and the fear that I would only get worse if I remained in the convent. She cursorily, mentioned that if I regained my health completely in one year, then I could be readmitted to the convent. I would find out later that the doctor had already told them that I would be dead within a few months! I was then told that they would call my family to prepare them for my homecoming. After lunch, the three of us went outside and

Throwaway Nun

Rosemary Scirocco-Corsale
Kathleen A. Barreca

walked around the porch. Before re-entering the back door, Mother Pietra took my right hand in hers and said, "When you put makeup on your face, put a little on your hands so they will not look so pale." That was one of the few times in 11 years that Mother Pietra had spoken to me with any degree of gentleness and softness. I was not positively impressed! When we were in the hallway, she told me to go for a nap. I went to the third floor, but I did not sleep. So, I wrote:

"June, 1958. This is it. Mother Pietra told me that I am going home. I just can't continue with religious life. The doctor even said I have to go for my own sake. I can't seem to get better somehow and being home with no daily schedule, lots of rest, I have a good chance of getting better again. Mother Pietra has faith I will be better in a year. It's awful to return again. I wish I could disappear, but I have to face every inch of this sacrifice. This is God's will, so be it done. Tomorrow I go to the hospital for blood transfusions and after that it will be a waiting of anguish for my vows to expire on June 30. Then, home to stay. Mother Pietra gave me faith and courage to do God's will. It is really what He wants. My family is resenting it bitterly, but it's up to me to see it through for myself and for them. Prove to them I am happy to do God's will, to offer this sacrifice for His glory. Show them the bit of good spirit in things I learn here at the convent, and carry that spirit always with me. Smile and speak nice even if inside your heart is being ripped to pieces; and, in the secret of your heart, offer the sacrifices to God. Be of service to everyone. Pray always and be good, and perhaps God will grant you the grace you need."

So, the die was cast! My mind raced, but it did not focus on going back into the secular world. Rather, it remained like a movie film that recalled so many things as vividly as when they occurred or whenever the

Throwaway Nun

Rosemary Scirocco-Corsale
Kathleen A. Barreca

words were spoken. I wondered if other postulants and nuns were also sent out for other than "holy" reasons....for example, if they were not liked by Mother Pietra. I wondered what was going on one day when I walked into Mother Pietra's bedroom and saw Sr. Clara seated on her lap—feeling and stroking her flat chest! I wondered why there was a special "something" between Mother Pietra and Sr. Constance! I wondered why there was so much hair on Mother Pietra's hands and arms! Although many European women have some facial hair, it seemed that Mother Pietra had more than the usual! I wondered why her voice was so deep! Something was wrong! It would be years before I could put a name to it, was it possible that Mother Pietra was a hermaphrodite with predominant male characteristics? I was horrified all over again! I was surprised by what happened next. While all these things kept running through my mind, I felt a calming peace come over me. I felt my stomach unravel for the first time in years! I felt as though a hand had come over me and stilled the "rough waters." My mind had become blank; I could no longer think. At that moment, I was called from my nap—I had been in my bed for over two hours.

From that time onward, Sr. Jerald never said an unkind word to me. If Sr. Jerald didn't speak harshly to me, neither did anyone else. In fact, there seemed to be a concerted effort to treat me kindly. Perhaps they wanted these kindnesses to be remembered instead of the 11 years of ugliness I suffered. I was told that it was for my health. I never again ate raw liver, and when the other nuns cooked liver for me, it was well done. I no longer cooked my dinner, and often, I was permitted to eat less by just asking permission. In the mornings, I would be given a sweet roll instead of having to force down two slices of dry bread. I was given chicken,

Throwaway Nun   Rosemary Scirocco-Corsale
Kathleen A. Barreca

ground beef, and veal with varied vegetables, and I was very grateful. Since my hospital stay, I had been permitted to go out canvassing three times. Each of these times seemed to have a different effect on me. I now looked at how women were dressed and what they wore on their feet. I looked at their makeup. I read the myriads of advertisements on the subways and buses. I looked at the secular world for the first time in 11 years; it was somewhat baffling!

On June 25, 1958, my vows had expired and I was, for all intents and purposes, no longer Sr. Mary Carmel—I was simply Rosemary. I sadly fully wrote:

"July 1, 1958. While there are hearts beating with jubilation and joy, there is one breaking with sorrow; if only I could understand why God permitted this.

But I can just say, "Lead kindly light, lead Thou me on."

Regardless of what, if my vows expire, my heart doesn't, and I will want my full consecration. However, I continued to wear the habit and to be called by my religious name. Within days, a Postulant, Theresa, came to the convent in Staten Island. One afternoon, we were in the chapel for a visit to the Blessed Sacrament, and we were alone. She proceeded to tell me that she was being sent home because the nuns had discovered that she suffered from petit mal, a mild form of epilepsy. I told her that I, too, was being sent home. She looked at me and her jaw dropped. When she recovered from her surprise, she asked me what the reason was. I told her that I had been very sick for the past two years and that the Order no longer wanted me in the convent. (*There in the small chapel we exchanged home addresses. We promised to write to one another once we were settled "in the world." We did so for several years. Theresa got married*

Throwaway Nun

**Rosemary Scirocco-Corsale
Kathleen A. Barreca**

and we lost touch.) The very next day, Theresa was driven to her parents' home in the New York Bronx area. A few days later, it would be my turn. On July 3, 1958, I was told to go to the infirmary where I was to find clothing to wear. It was after lunch, and I was told that I would leave for home that day. I undressed slowly, kissing each piece of the habit which I would never wear again! The dress that I was to wear was the same as that of a postulant. It had been sewn of a thick, taffeta-type material. I was given a pair of under panties, but no bra (*I did not need one because I had very small breasts*). I was to keep on my black stockings and wear a pair of wedge-heeled shoes similar to those worn by women in the 1940's. The shoes were white and made with cloth on top which was glossed with white polish. I was given a blue sweater. My hair was in braids which were crossed over the top of my head. I felt that I looked hideously, and that I belonged to some sect. I came down the steps and was met by Sr. Jerald. We were home alone at the time. She told me to return upstairs until I was called. She gave me an old suitcase into which I was instructed to place the towels and handkerchiefs which had been placed on my bed. At four o'clock, I was called to the first floor where Sr. Jerald told me that it was time to go. The station wagon was just outside the back door. I got in on the passenger side and never looked back! Sr. Jerald drove to a gas station on St. George Boulevard to fill the tank. The service attendant said, "Have a nice day, Sisters," and Sr. Jerald burst out crying, struggling hard to muffle the sob. She drove away to the ferryboat dock. Neither of us said anything; I don't think I would have spoken even if I had been given the latitude to speak. At the Pennsylvania Station in New York City, I was taken to the gate where the train would depart. I would arrive in Youngstown the next day. When the gate opened to allow the passengers

Throwaway Nun

Rosemary Scirocco-Corsale
Kathleen A. Barreca

to board, Sr. Jerald walked with me to the boarding car. She thrust $25 in my hand and told me that they had not been able to reserve a berth for me and the money was for me to try to get one if I could. She told me to send the money back if I did not use it. Needless to say, the train was full. I spent the night in the ladies' restroom; I was unable to sleep. By the time I reached Youngstown the next morning, I was physically exhausted. I was met at the train station by two nuns with a station wagon (I can only remember one of them—Sr. Angelica who had come from Italy). I was told that I would have to wait until they picked up some boxes at the baggage claim. As usual, the nuns in Staten Island did not miss a beat to use this opportunity to send many boxes of books, religious articles, and statuary to the nuns here. Not even this tragic occasion would stop them in their opportunism. I was taken directly to my parents' home. They had received a call from Staten Island advising them of my arrival time. As I started up the stairs to the front door, both shoes tore apart; the cloth fabric tore away from the soles. Under the white polish was rotting, brown cloth. Sr. Angelica told me not to worry because my parents would buy me new shoes. I was greeted warmly by my parents. It was apparent that both of them had spent many days and nights worrying about me. Their eyes were very sad and they spoke with hushed tones. More than once I felt my mother was about to burst out in tears, but she maintained control. My father asked why the Order refused his offer to pay all of the medical expenses rather than send me home. This question floored me! I was told that there were several telephone calls between my parents and Mother Pietra. A few weeks later, I would learn that my parents were told by the convent that they did not want a funeral! Sr. Angelica said very little. It was apparent that she was very uncomfortable. She referred my parents

Throwaway Nun

**Rosemary Scirocco-Corsale
Kathleen A. Barreca**

back to Mother Pietra for answers to their questions. In a few minutes, the nuns were gone. For the first time in 11 years, I stood alone in a world I had left behind. For the first time, I regretted the fact that I was not dead! Dead had to be better than this!

The very next day, my sister brought me to the family physician, Dr. G. Frye. When he entered the examining room, my sister introduced us and said that I had just gotten home from the convent, and that I was anemic. The doctor told my sister in front of me that he didn't need to be told that; he could see it in my eyes. Without taking down any medical information or asking any questions, he told my sister that I was very sick and should be hospitalized immediately. He instructed his nurse to call St. Elizabeth's Hospital in Youngstown, Ohio, to inform them that my sister would be bringing me in. Later that evening, she would return to bring me some nightgowns, a robe, and two bed jackets. I was very unaccustomed to the feeling of silky apparel next to my skin. I felt so naked and I wore the bed jackets at all times.

By the early afternoon of my hospital admission, I was receiving my first blood transfusion. Between the three transfusions I had received at St. Anthony's Hospital in Long Island, NY, just three weeks prior and the seven transfusions I would get at St. Elizabeth's Hospital during the next three weeks, there was no question that I was very seriously ill. The bleeding ulcerative colitis was taking its toll. Members of my family visited every day. My sister was sure to call once or twice a day if she were unable to come during visiting hours.

Doctor Frye came every morning. On the second day, he told me that he was calling in a specialist, a proctologist named Dr. Harold. I had very limited experience with medical personnel; however, it seemed to me

Throwaway Nun

Rosemary Scirocco-Corsale
Kathleen A. Barreca

that both attending physicians were very attentive and concerned. The nursing staff was extremely caring and gentle. I was amazed at my meal regimen; I enjoyed all of my meals. I would never again eat the foods as in the convent!

There were several medical tests and examinations that I underwent during those first ten days in the hospital. I was still bleeding rectally, but the spasms in my stomach abated. I felt no more tightness. The constant nausea was gone. The rash behind my ears was also improving, although the scabs across my scalp persisted. The doctors questioned the large areas of my upper arms and buttocks which were permanently discolored. This was the direct result of the incorrect manner with which I was given my daily injections of Inferon, a strong source of iron for my anemia. On several occasions, large groups of young interns as well as smaller groups accompanying the attending physicians would come to my beside. Later, I would be told that there was no known case of anyone surviving two years of exacerbated bleeding ulcerative colitis. The doctors were sometimes playful; they would ask me to lift up my sleeves so the young interns could try to figure out why I was "two-toned." The discoloration was very brown and stood in contrast with the pale, white skin around it. When I understood the game, I would smile and tell them that I was born two-toned. Dr. Harold told me that I was the first case he had ever treated with such severe results of incorrectly given intramuscular injections. He explained that I was a very good "teaching subject." I readily complied; after all, I did not know what disobedience or refusal was!

As a result of my condition, the attending physicians held a conference with the medical staff of the hospital and presented my case.

Throwaway Nun

Rosemary Scirocco-Corsale
Kathleen A. Barreca

Dr. Frye was the first to come to tell me what the treatment options were for my condition. The consensus of opinions was that I would have to undergo surgery as quickly as possible. Dr. Harold favored a colostomy wherein an opening would be made in the large intestine or bowel with a connection to the outside of my body; I would have a bag for elimination attached to my lower abdomen. I would have to be taught how to empty the bag and how to care for myself. Another surgical option was an ileotomy, which was making an opening for elimination higher up the intestine to accommodate the diseased colon. After Dr. Frye had presented these alternatives, he said the decision was mine. I answered simply; I refused any form of surgery. Dr. Frye accepted my decision although he stated he couldn't see any hope for a good outcome without surgery. Still, I refused. In the next three days, I was visited by the Catholic chaplain, the Director of Nursing (who was a nun), and the Associate Director of the hospital (also a nun). They all tried to convince me to agree to surgery. Father Lange, the Catholic chaplain, was the most forthright. He asked if I knew what I faced without surgery. I said I understood that I would die. The others shook their heads and left my room. Father Lange took my hand in his and said that he would pray for me so that I might make my decision with discernment; and that it was really the will of God. He gave me his blessing and left the room. In my solitude, I knew that my decision was the right one, but I could not explain why. Dr. Frye, I later learned, defended my decision and held everyone else at bay.

My family never lost their faith and continued their daily prayers. On July 16, 1958, which is the religious feast day of the Mother of Jesus, commonly known as Our Lady of Mount Carmel, I suddenly stopped bleeding! Carmel had been my name in religion, and it was my sister's

Throwaway Nun

Rosemary Scirocco-Corsale
Kathleen A. Barreca

name. I cannot deny Divine intervention; I just know that on that day I stopped bleeding and began to regain my strength. Dr. Harold was so incredulous that he performed a proctologic examination to determine "the truth," as he put it. He had been concerned that I was just telling everyone I had stopped bleeding only to avoid surgery. When he finished the exam, he shook his head and told me there was no longer any reason for anyone to hesitate in believing me. I had, in fact, stopped bleeding. I did not have surgery. However, I remained in the hospital because of the need for more blood transfusions. Dr. Frye said that I should be home by the end of the month.

It did not take long for the ten days to go by. One morning, the nurses removed the needle and other items associated with the transfusions. I was not to get any more blood. I was now well enough to go home with my parents. I had, after all, not died, and something deep inside of me told me that I would not see the end of my life at that time. That night is as vivid to me now as though it had just happened yesterday. I was resting in my bed when I became bothered and concerned about my future. I could feel my stomach tighten like it had done many times in the past. I could feel that I was fighting back tears and sobs. I felt helpless and hopeless. I did the only thing I knew how to do, I prayed. I prayed intensely and fervently. I prayed constantly. I was unable to sleep. At about two or two-thirty in the morning, I got out of bed, donned my robe, and sat in a chair by the window. I began to say the Rosary; I fingered every bead. Before I had finished, a nurse walked past my door. She retraced her steps and came into my room. She asked if I needed anything or if there was anything that she could do for me. I struggled to keep back my tears; I said that I could not sleep and that I had gotten up to say a few

Throwaway Nun

Rosemary Scirocco-Corsale
Kathleen A. Barreca

prayers. She looked and sounded genuinely concerned. Satisfied that all seemed well, she left the room and I continued with my prayers. When I was finished, I got up and stood in front of the window. At that time of the morning, all of the street lights were shining across the city. The window of my room faced the northwest side of town. For a moment, I wondered if any of those lights were shining on my hometown of Girard, Ohio, a few miles north. I had no way of knowing then; I had been gone so long. I stood looking outside for a very long time. I was absorbed in my thoughts. I recalled the misery of my life in the convent, all of the pain, suffering, and never being understood. I entered the convent at the age of thirteen, and here I stood eleven years later. I was twenty-four years old and knew nothing about the world that lay in the panoramic view of my window. I knew that I was at the most momentous crossroads of my life: I could continue being a victim for the remainder of my life, or I could give myself a chance to get to know that world. I concluded that I deserved a chance to know the big, wide world and to see if, indeed, there was some niche in it for me! I could feel the tightness leave me. I almost felt elated. I would choose to find out all about the world where the night lights now cast dark shadows. And, at that very moment, I decided that I would never be a throwaway again!

EPILOGUE

Beyond overwhelming odds, I survived! Once out of the convent, I never suffered from bleeding ulcerative colitis again. I have never had another episode of a spastic stomach. I have never again struggled with rashes behind my ears or across my scalp. I have never needed a blood transfusion. I was cured! I would come to learn that these medical problems were called psychosomatic, that is, having their origins in severe emotional trauma, stresses, and anger. According to my attending physicians, they were not aware of, either in their practices or in medical literature, anyone who has survived such a prolonged and serious case of bleeding ulcerative colitis. My almost instant cure just a few weeks after leaving the convent was a very pleasant surprise to me and to the significant others in my life. I have never denied the possibility of a miracle. So be it!

Contrary to how the nuns viewed my person and their thoughts of me as having no intelligence whatsoever, I enrolled at Youngstown (OH) University just six weeks after I was discharged from the hospital. After the first semester, I was placed on the Dean's List. I received my Bachelor of Arts, and received a fellowship to attend graduate school for one year in Florida. I completed my Master's degree *(in Social Work)* at the Ohio State University, Columbus, OH, in 1965. In subsequent years, I studied for my Doctoral degree. I held professional positions in my field, and was in private practice psychotherapy for over 11 years. I was not, after all, retarded as the nuns like to think of me! I never pursued either music or art because they are two fields which remain too close to my tragic past. I never needed them.

Throwaway Nun

Rosemary Scirocco-Corsale
Kathleen A. Barreca

My marriage to a very wonderful man crowned my life. I felt really gifted! Joe, my husband, would often say, "Our marriage is made in Heaven;" I believed that! When he passed away in 1994, he was, and always will be, an everlasting part of me.

In 1988, I was medically retired from my position with the Veteran's Administration after suffering a stroke. After my husband passed away, I moved back to Girard, Ohio, where I was born, where all the members of my family live, and where I continue to live independently and comfortably.

I was never a throwaway again—I made it!

Throwaway Nun

Rosemary Scirocco-Corsale
Kathleen A. Barreca

Throwaway Nun

Rosemary Scirocco-Corsale
Kathleen A. Barreca

Made in the USA
Middletown, DE
12 May 2017